Fairy Tales
COLORING BOOK
— RUSS FOCUS —

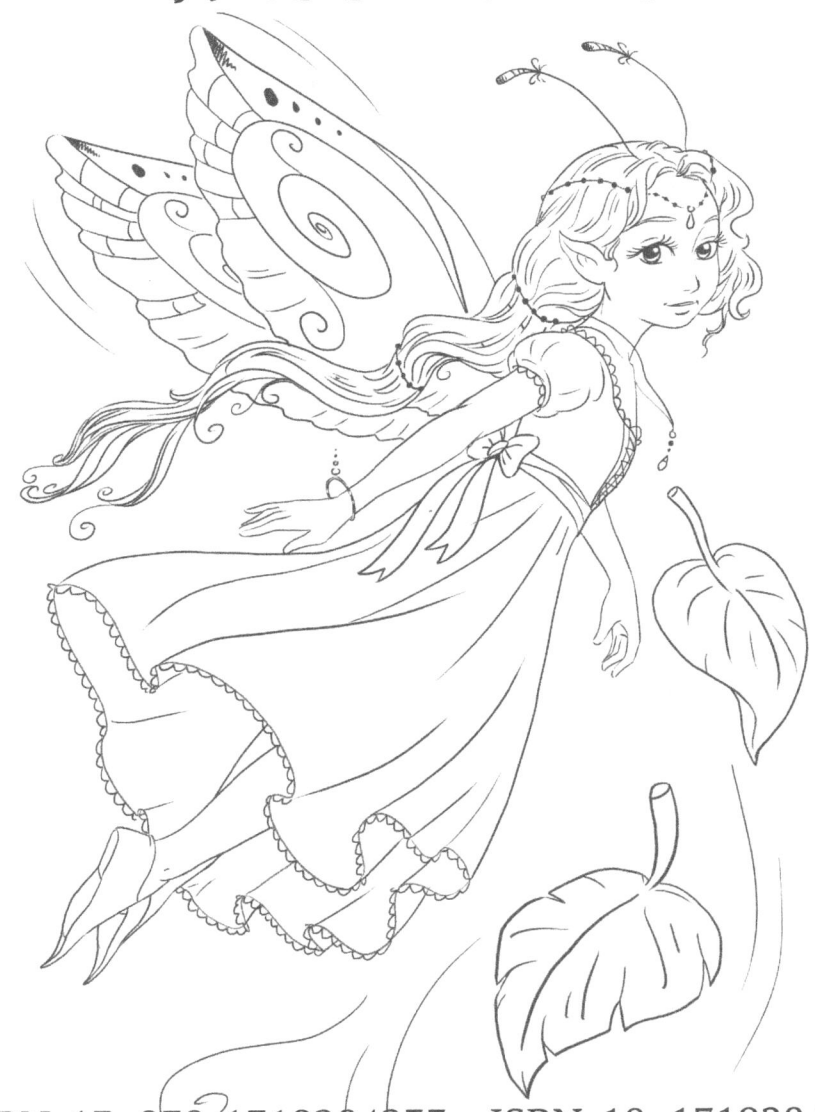

ISBN-13: 978-1719284233   ISBN-10: 1719284237
PUBLISHED BY RUSS FOCUS COPYRIGHT © 2018 ALL RIGHTS RESERVED

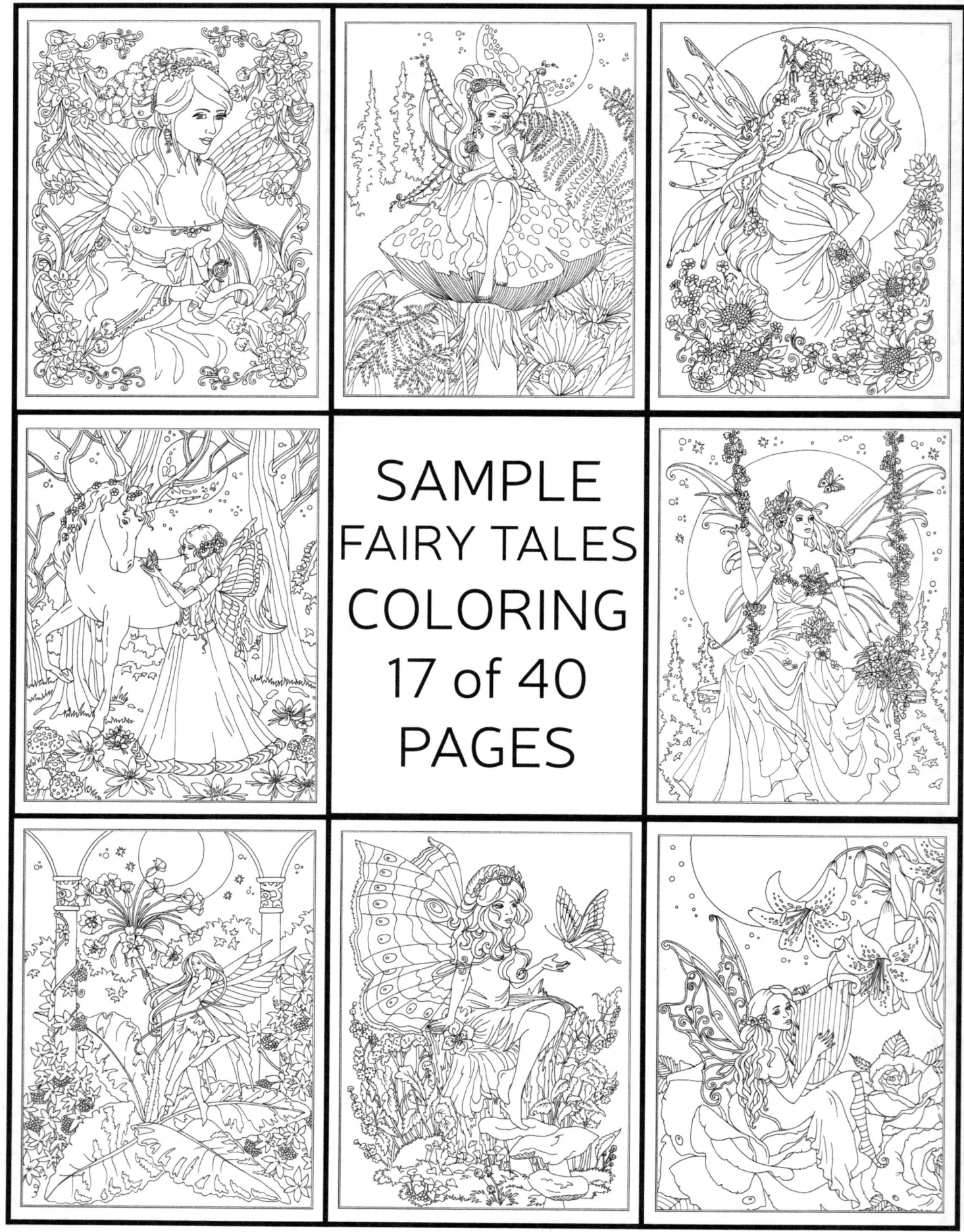

SAMPLE
FAIRY TALES
COLORING
17 of 40
PAGES

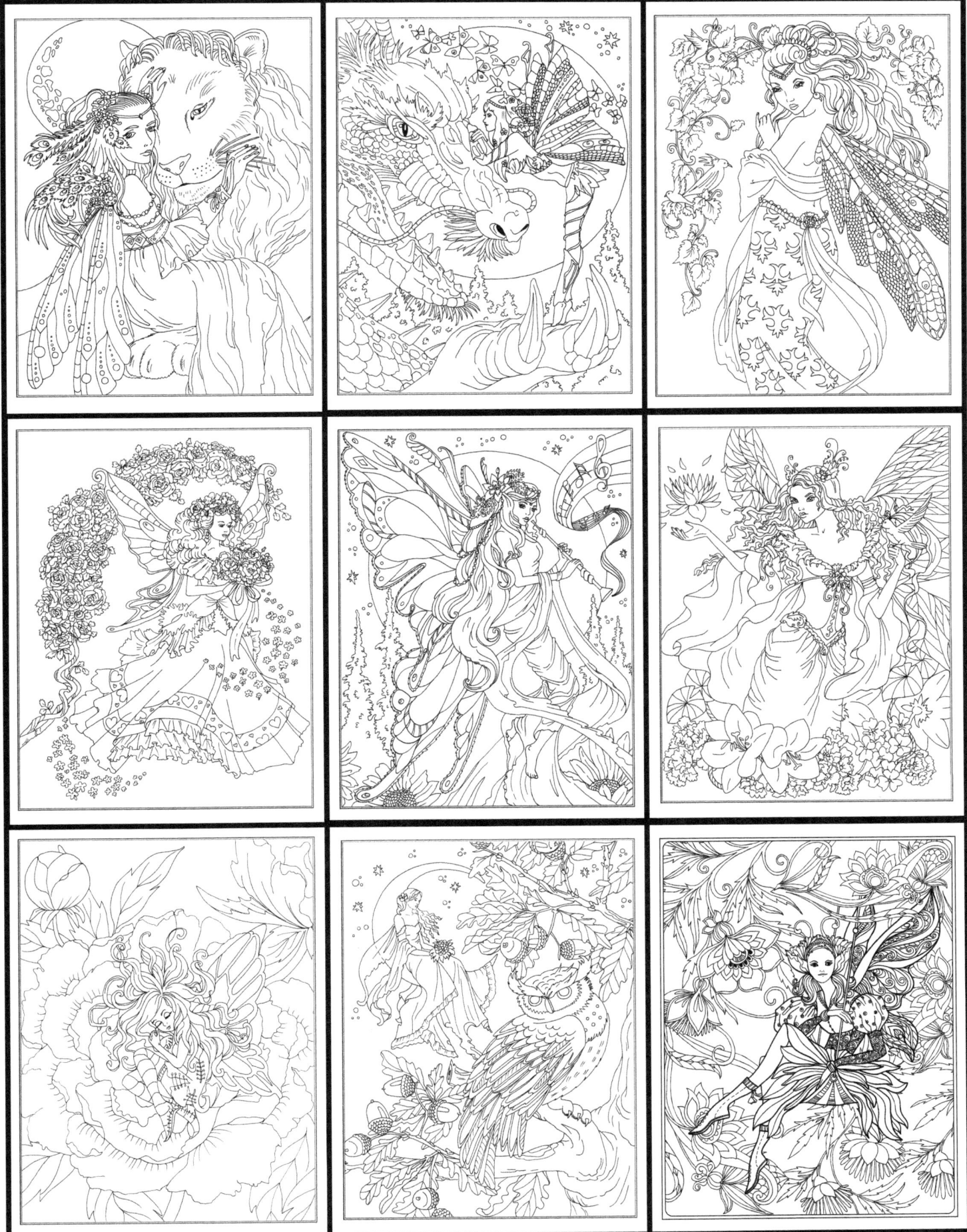

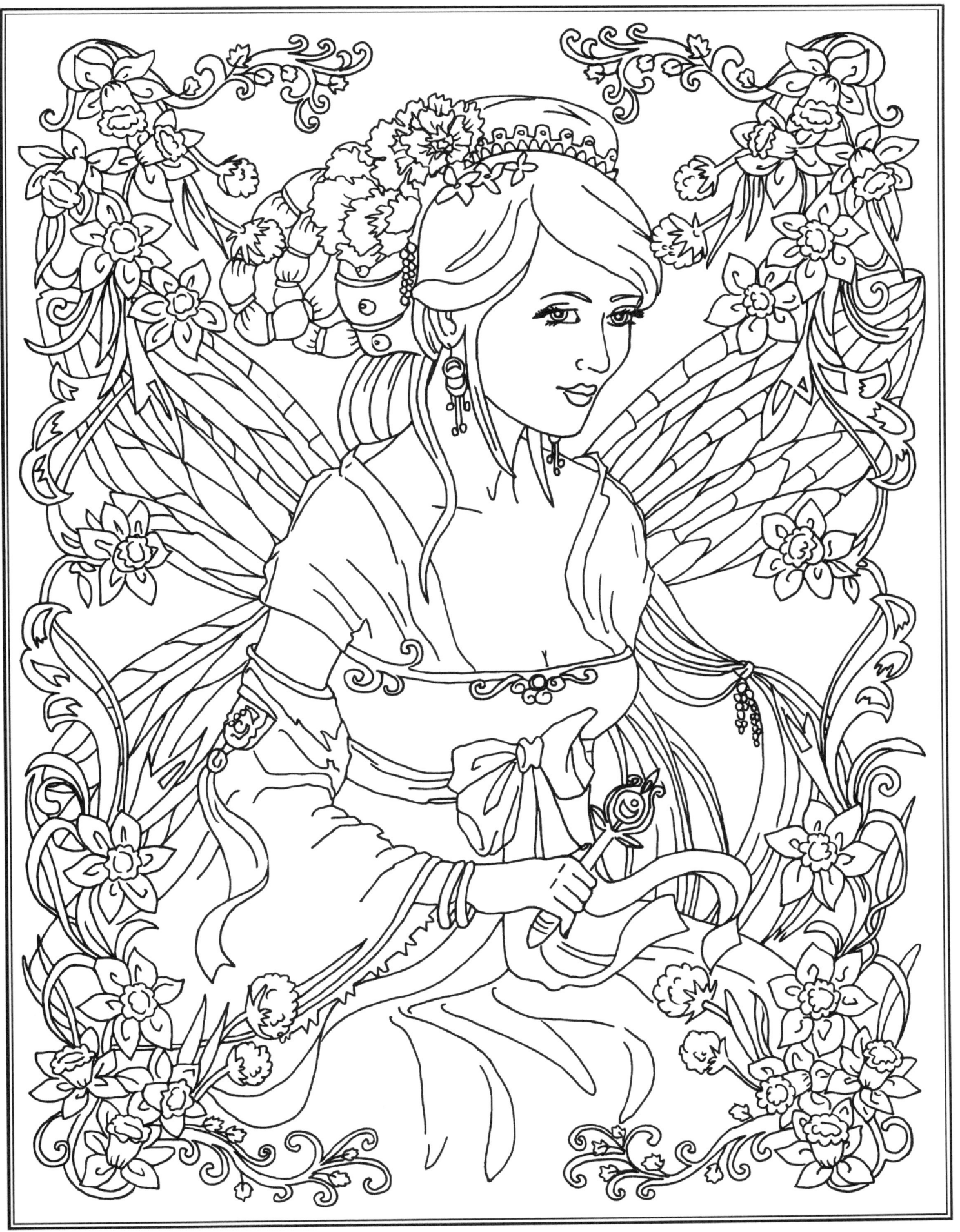

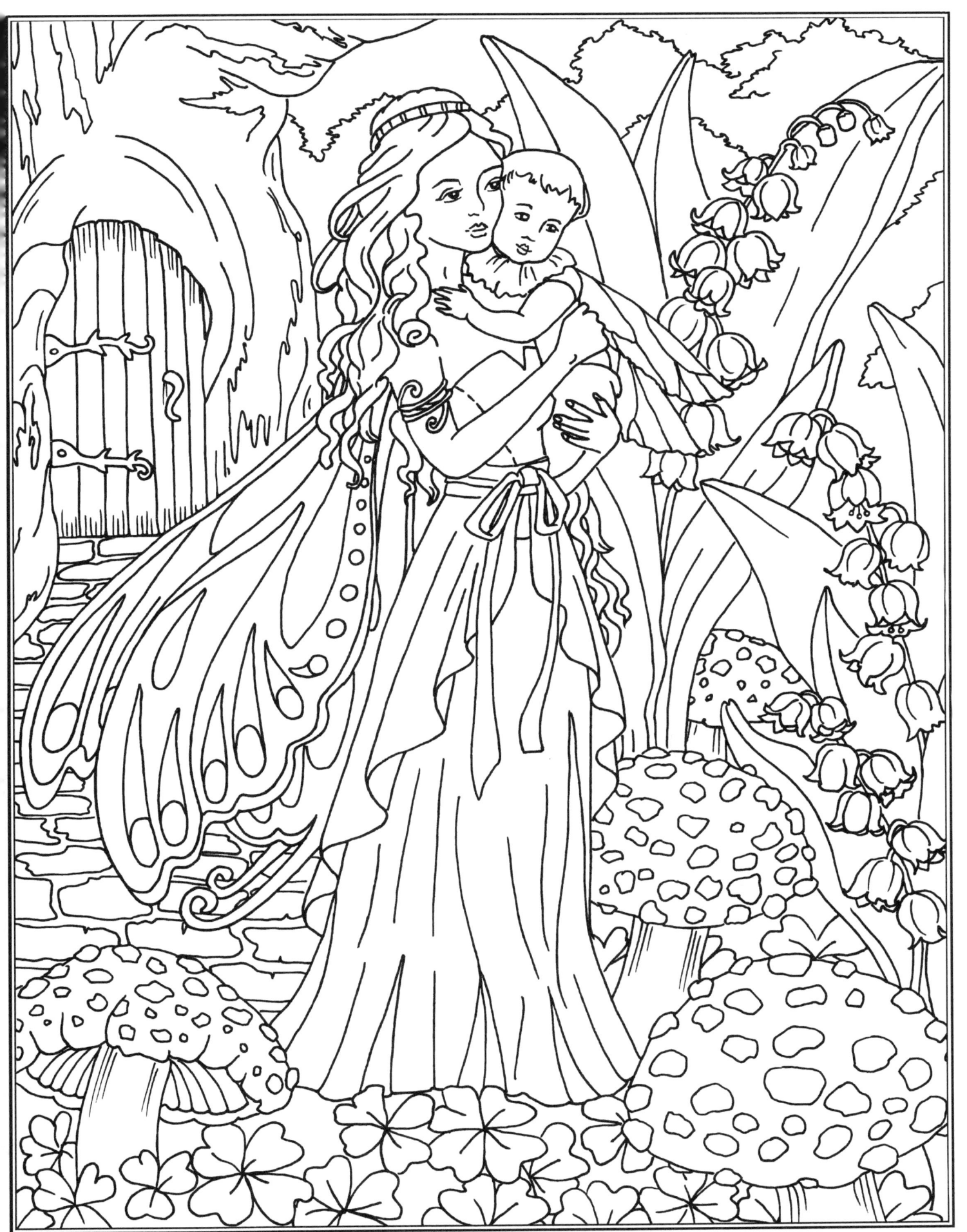

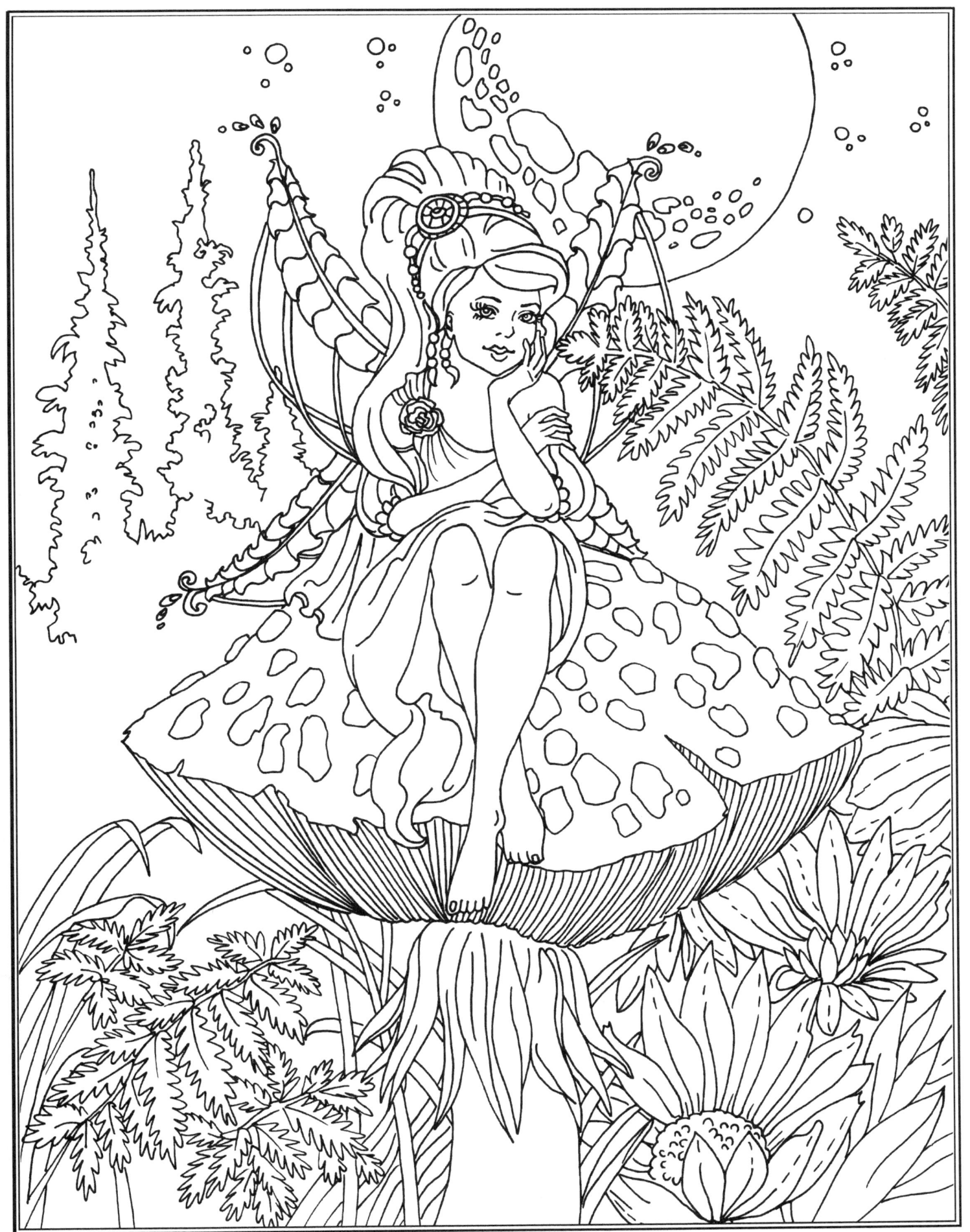

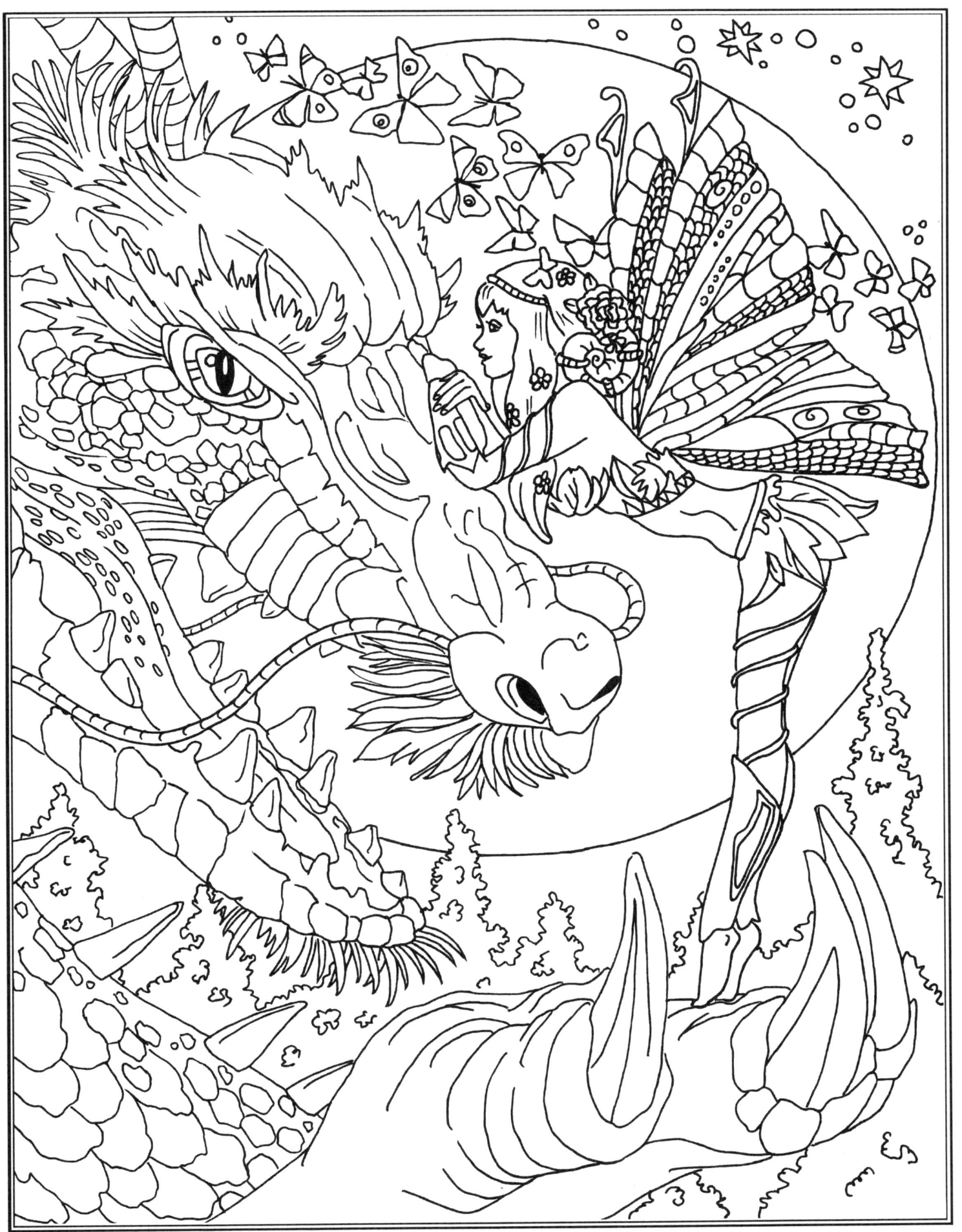

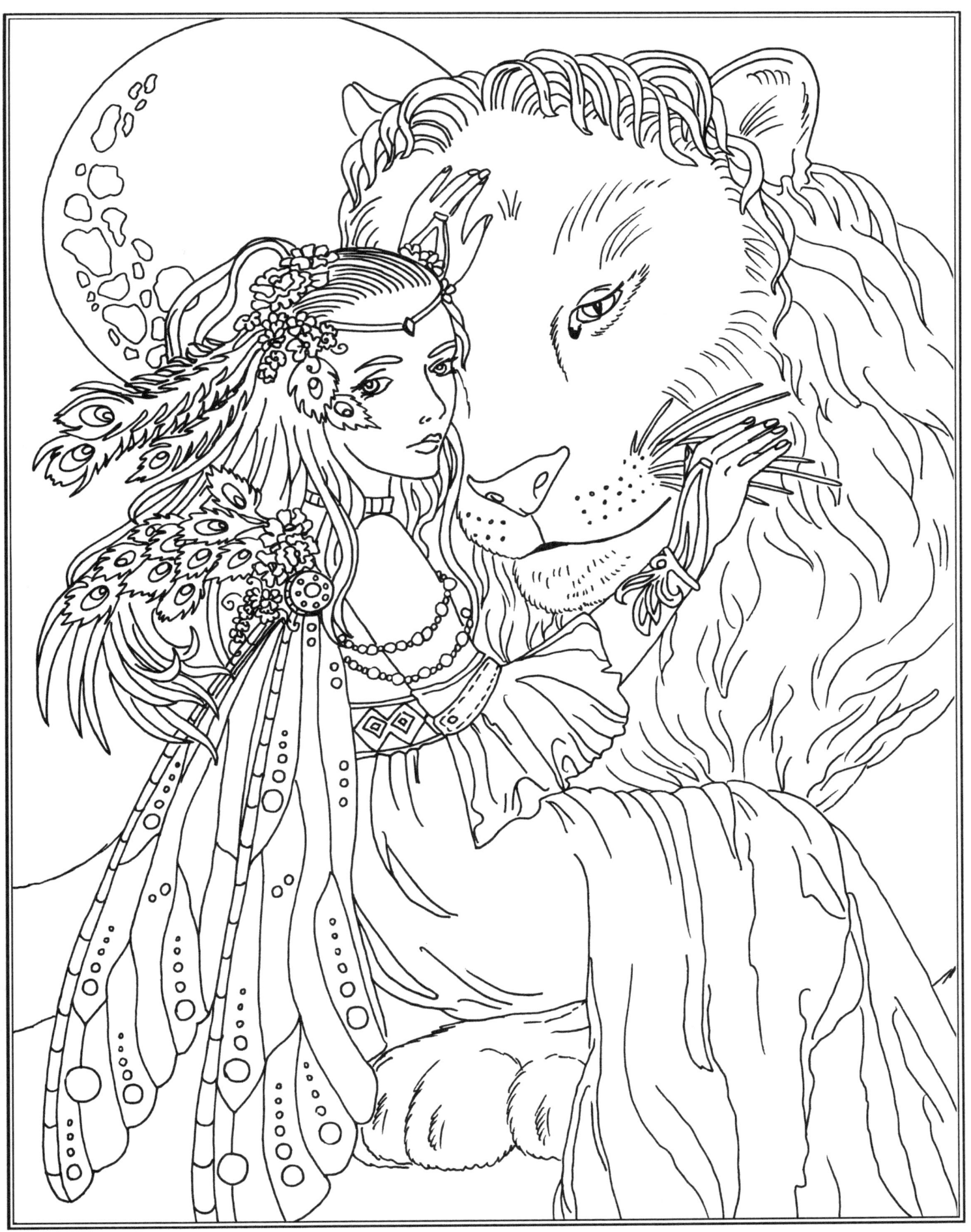

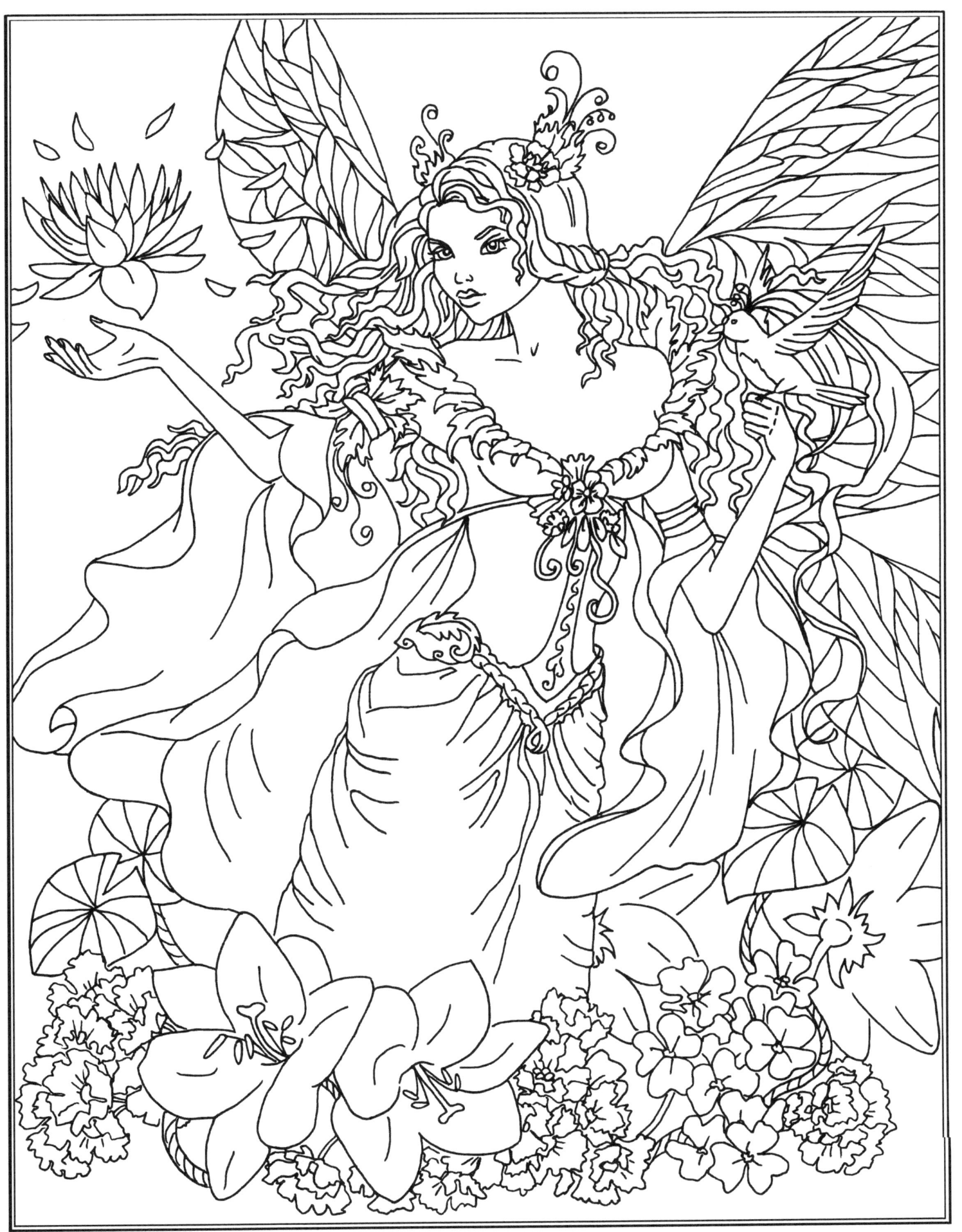

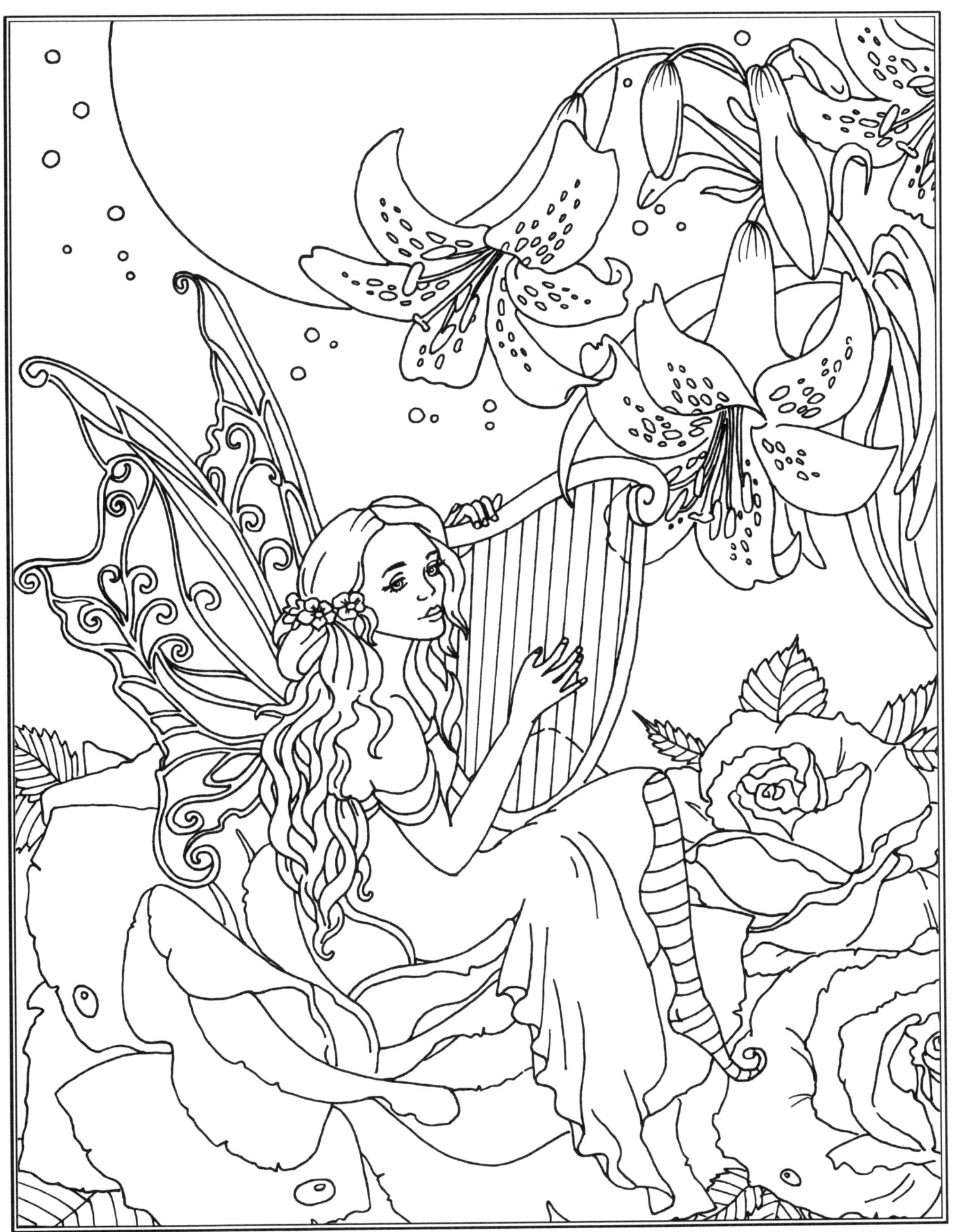

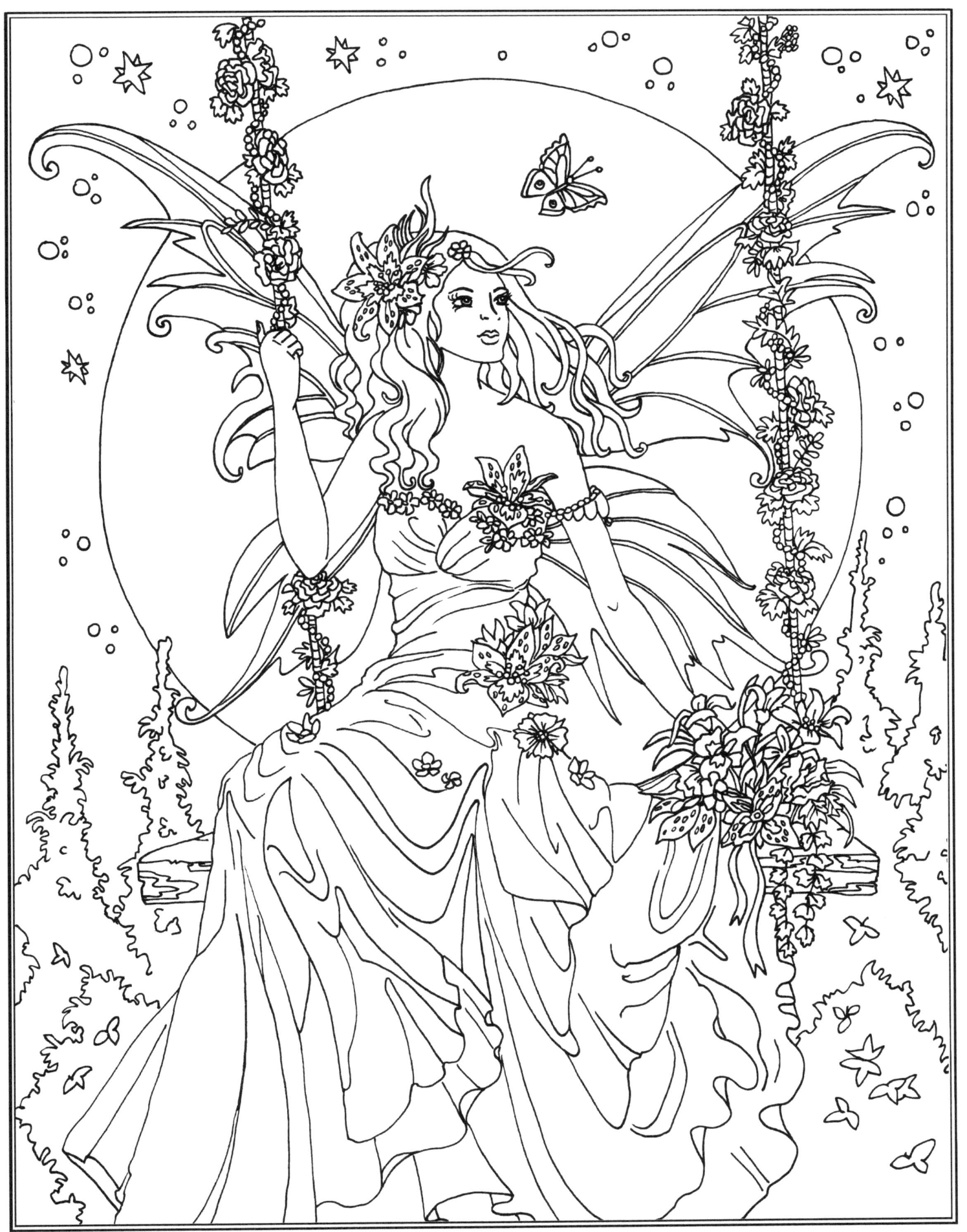

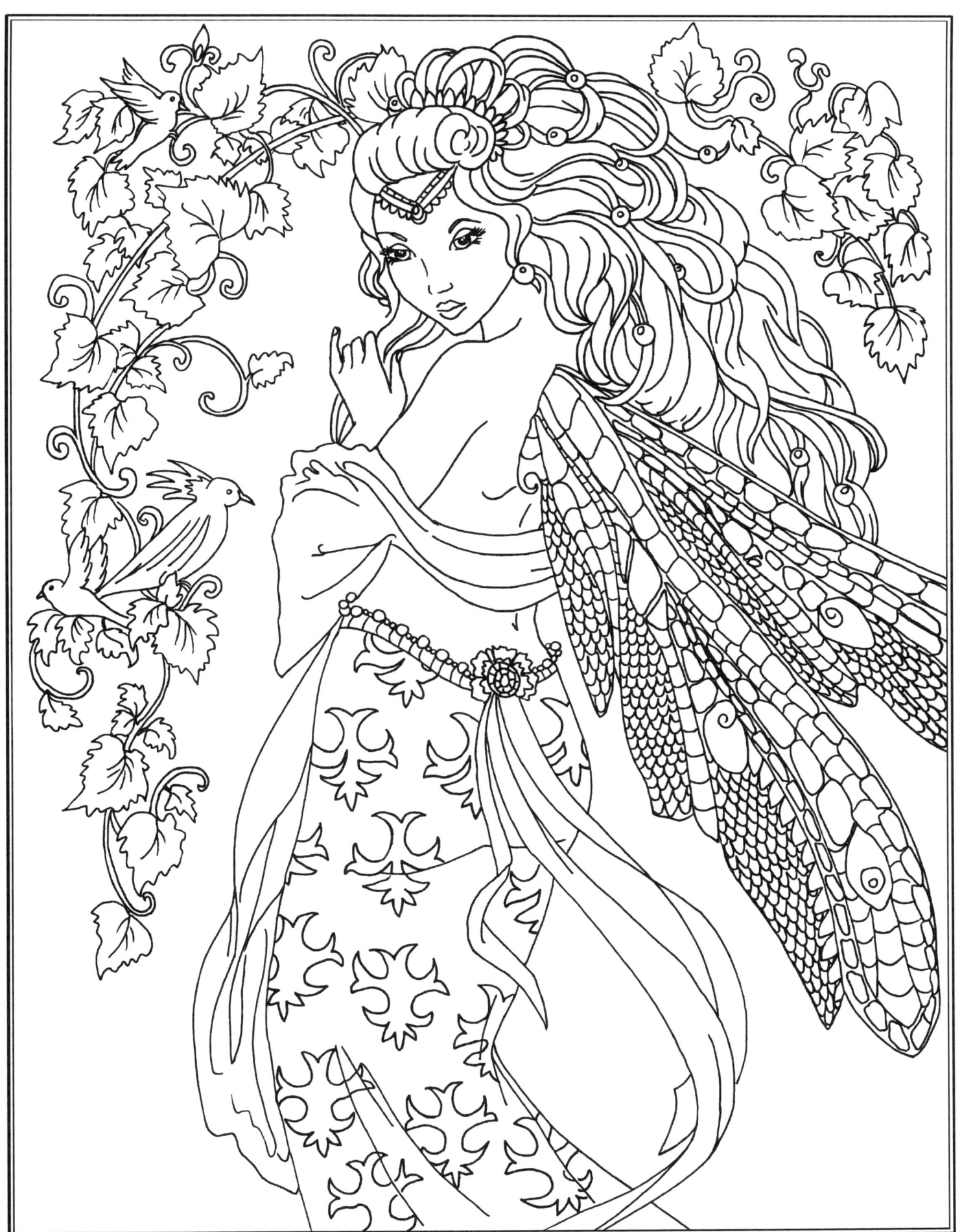

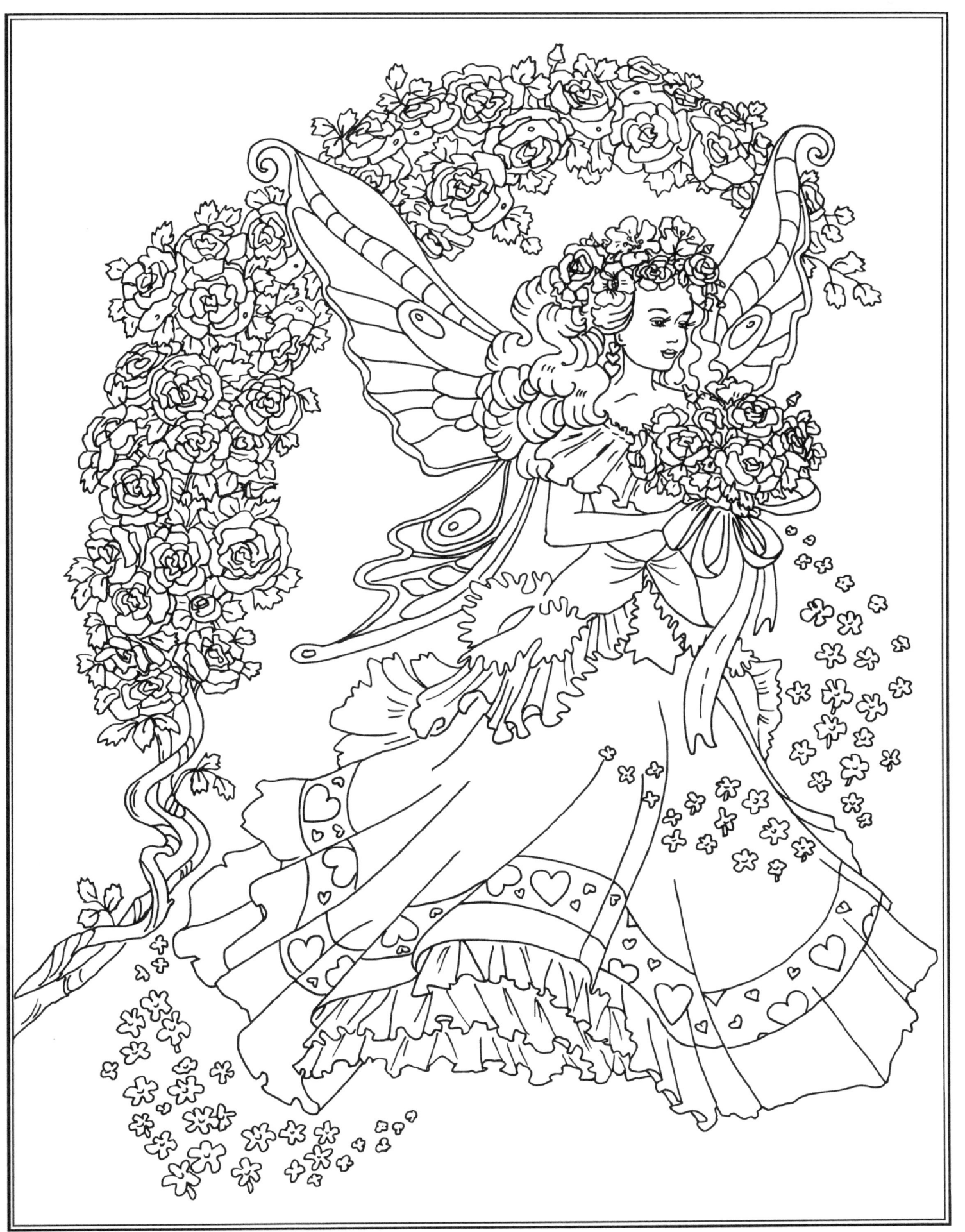

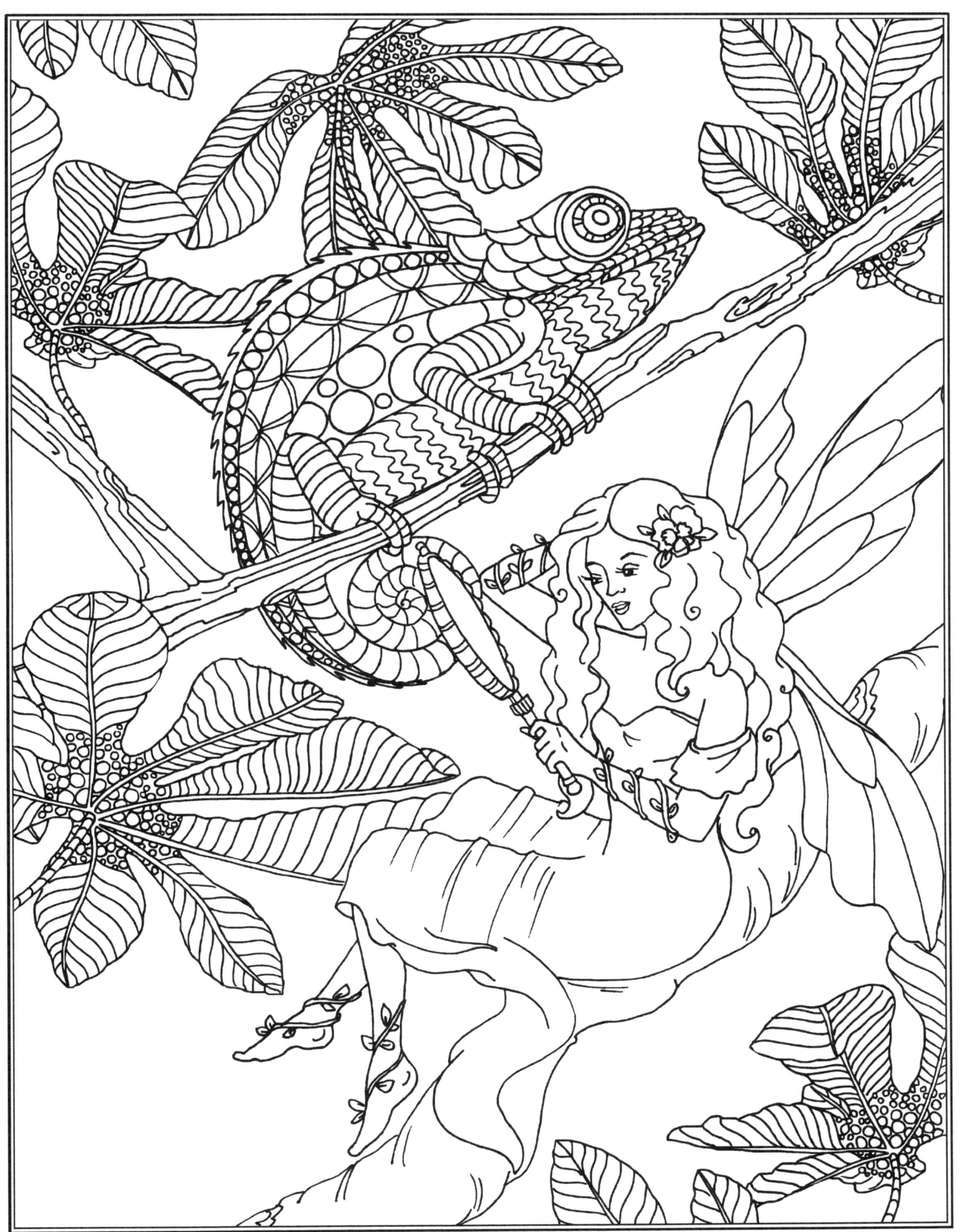

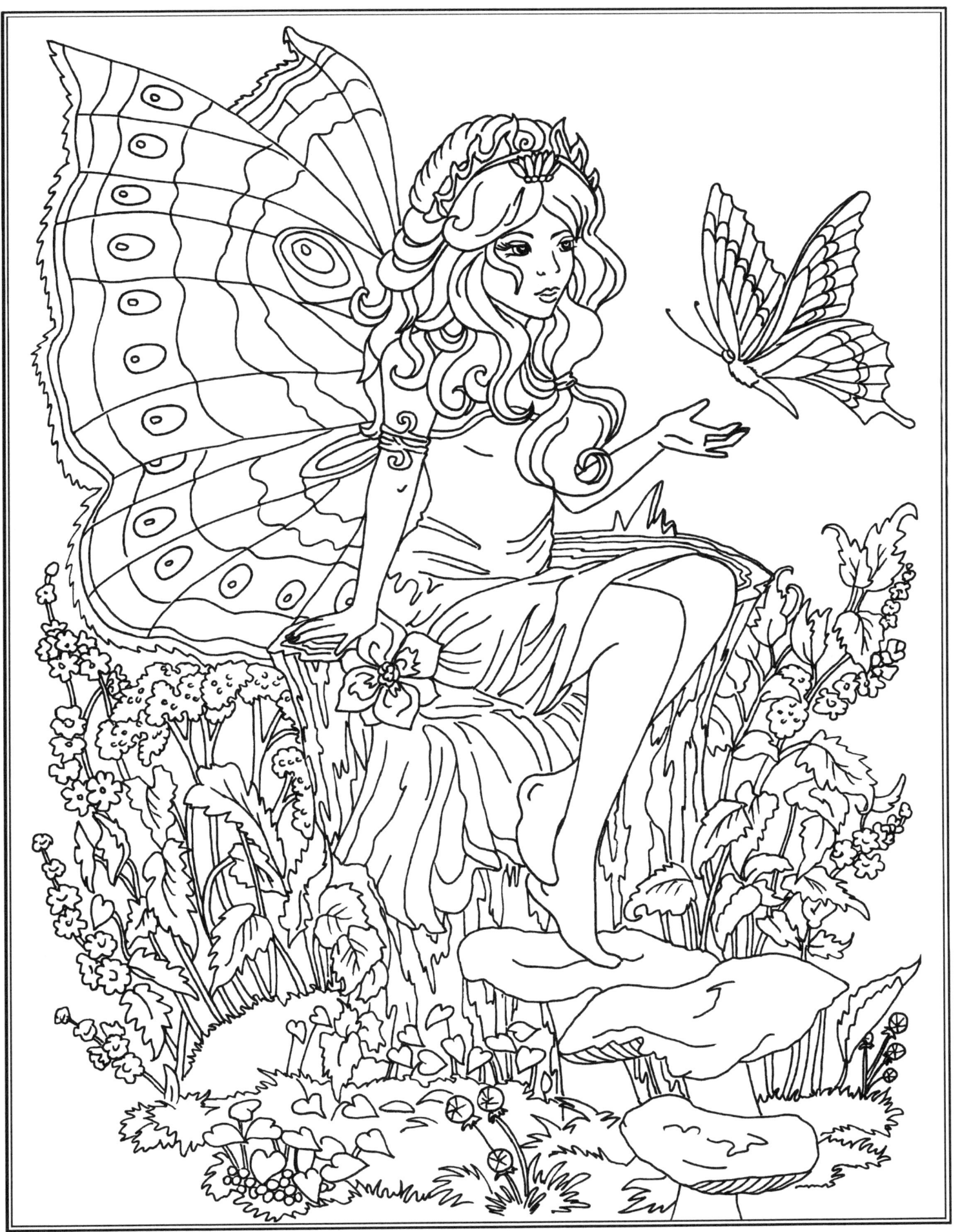

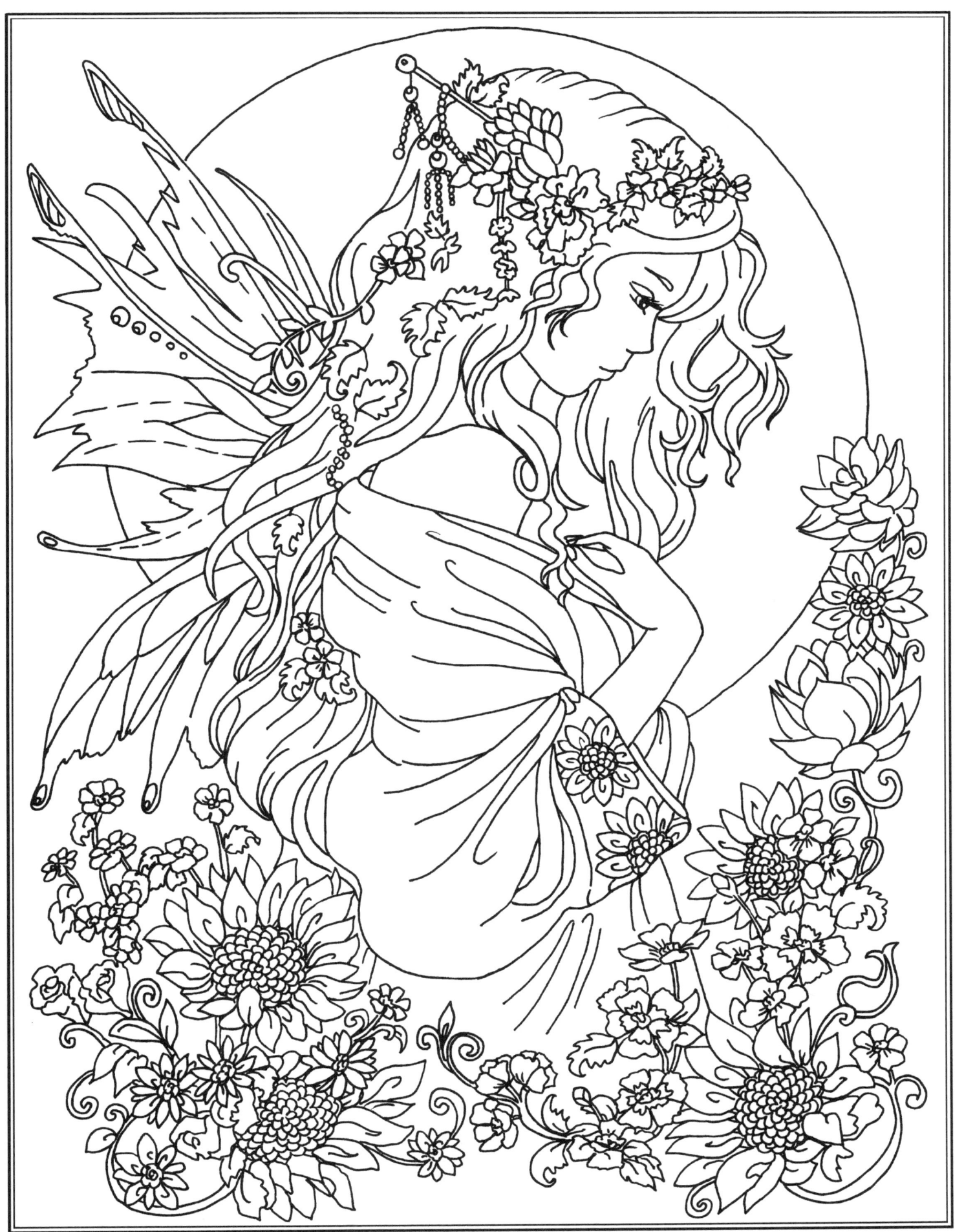

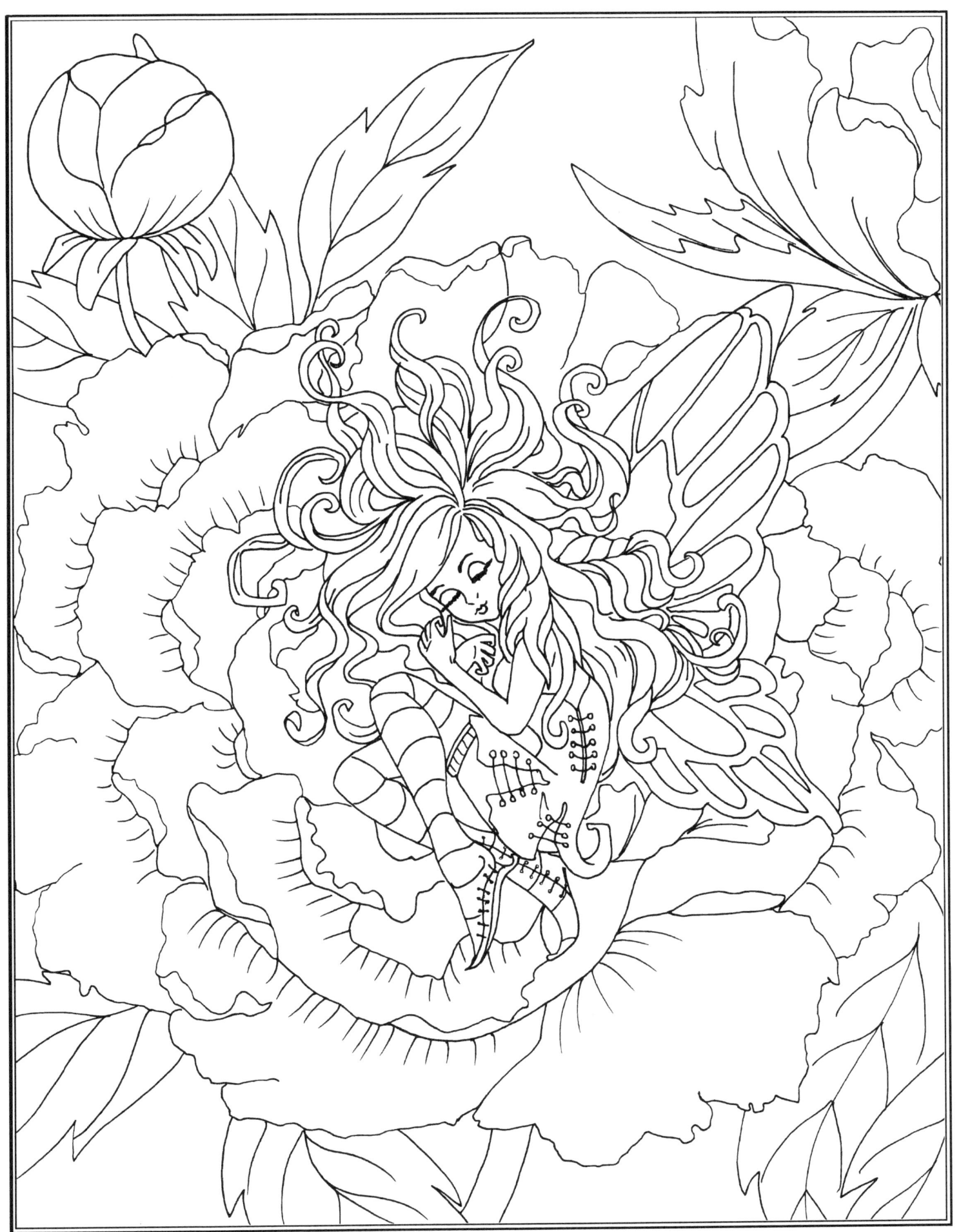

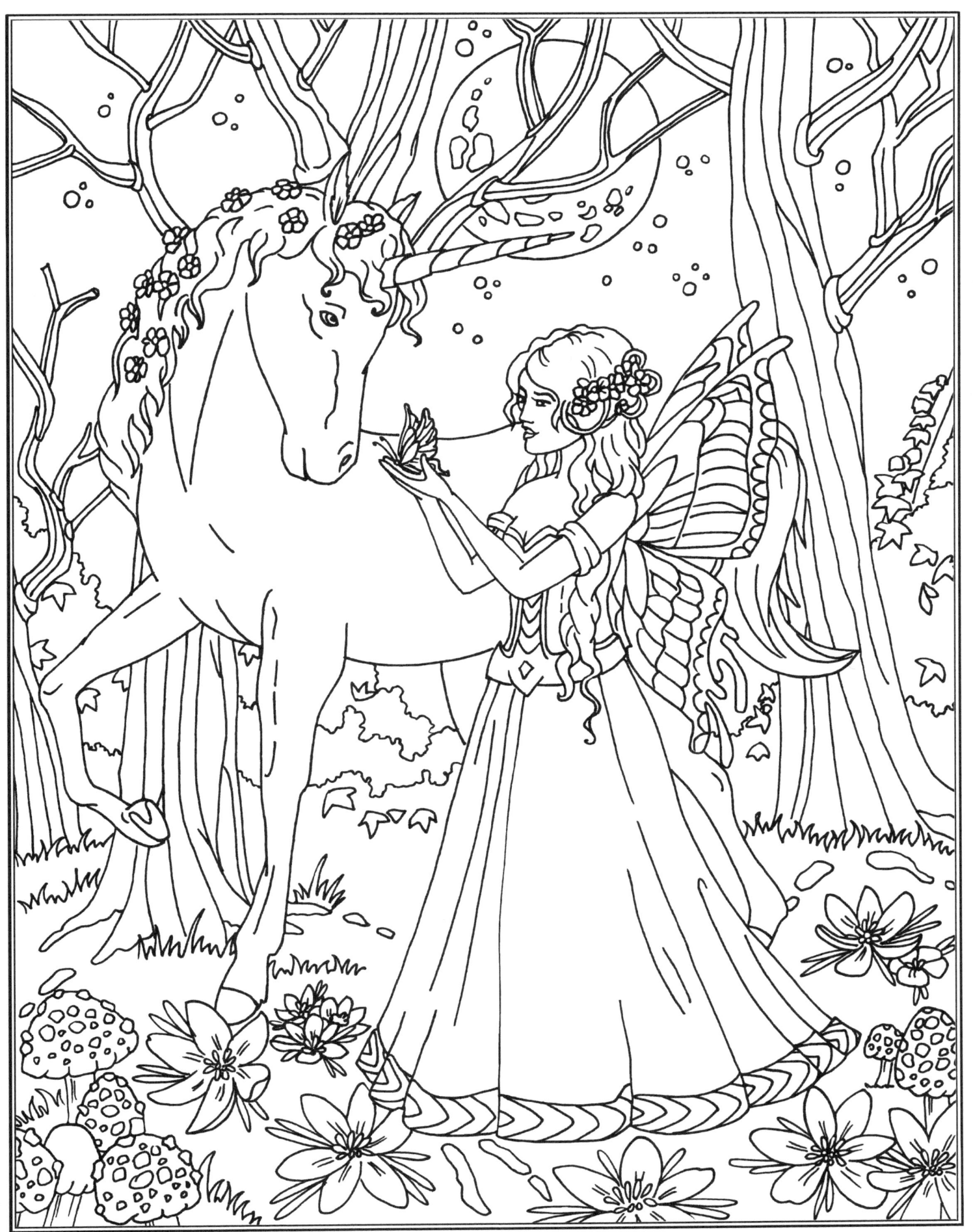

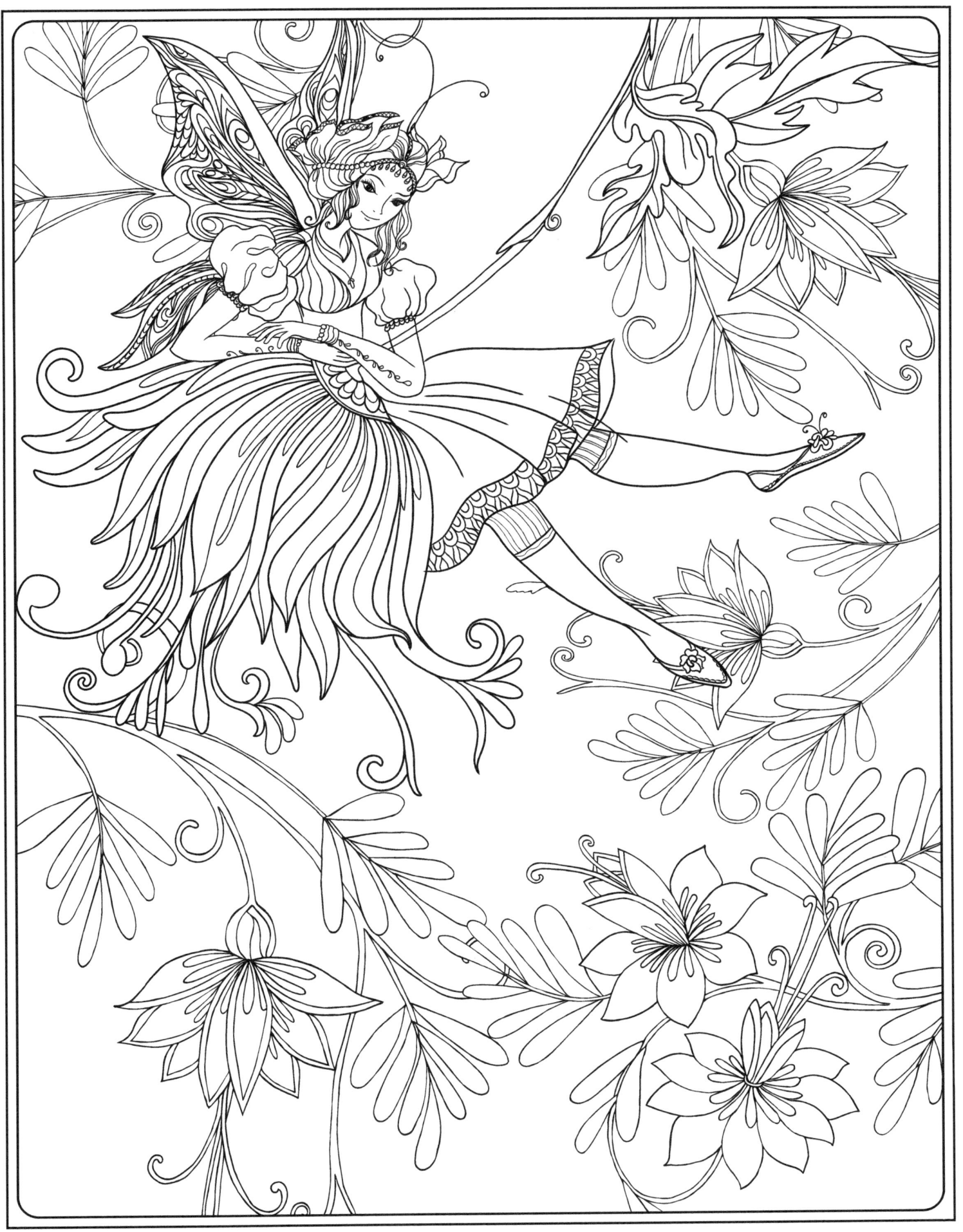

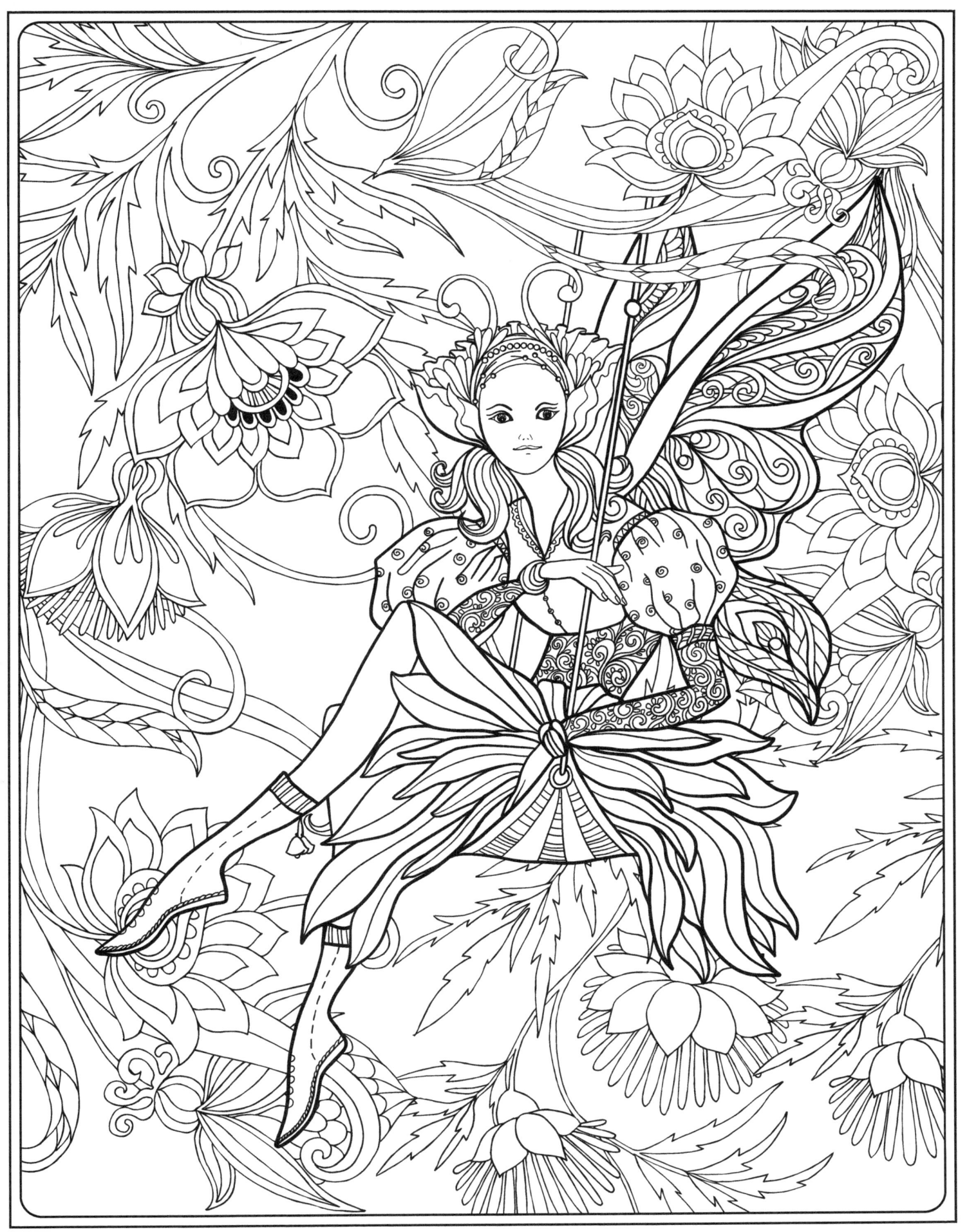

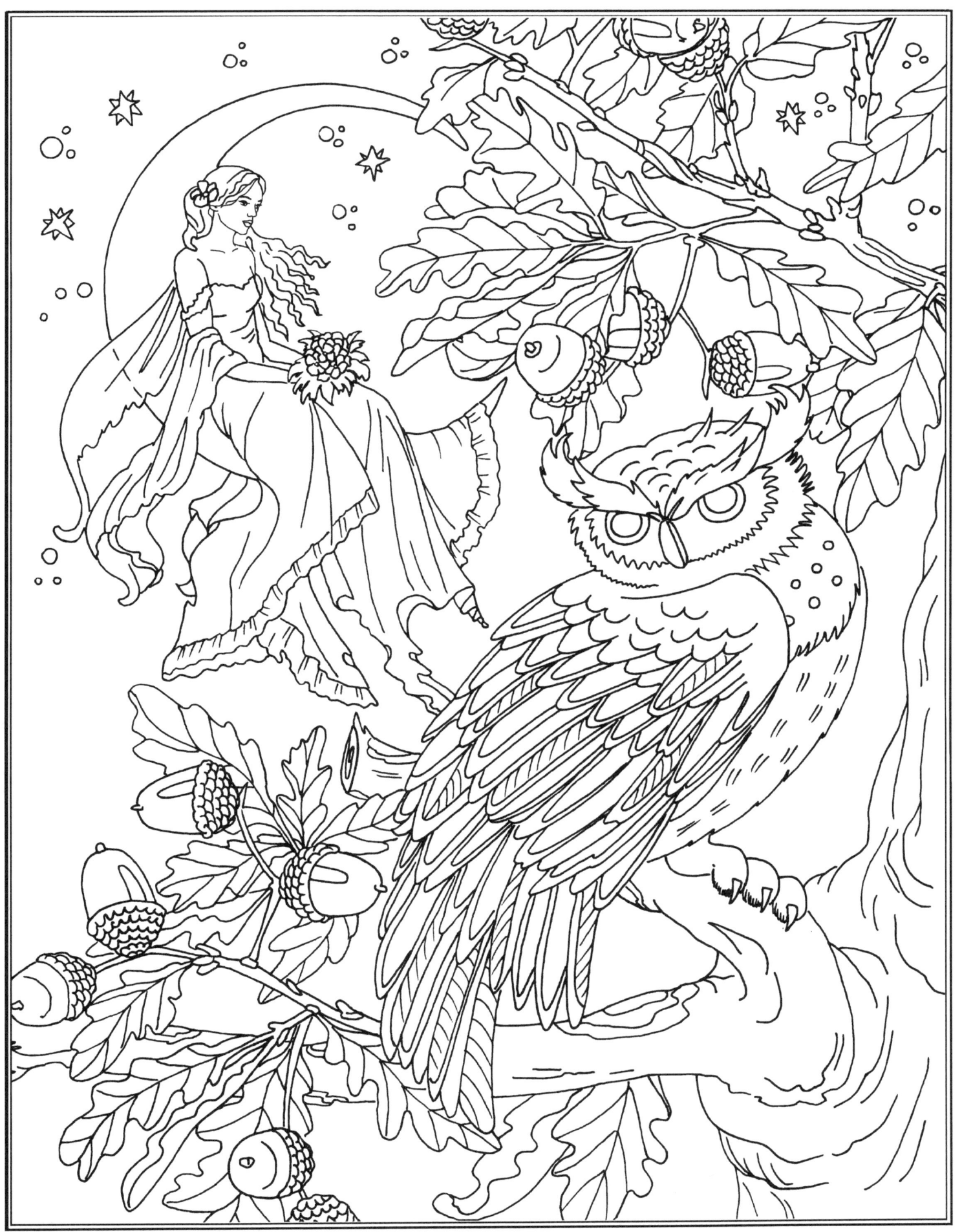

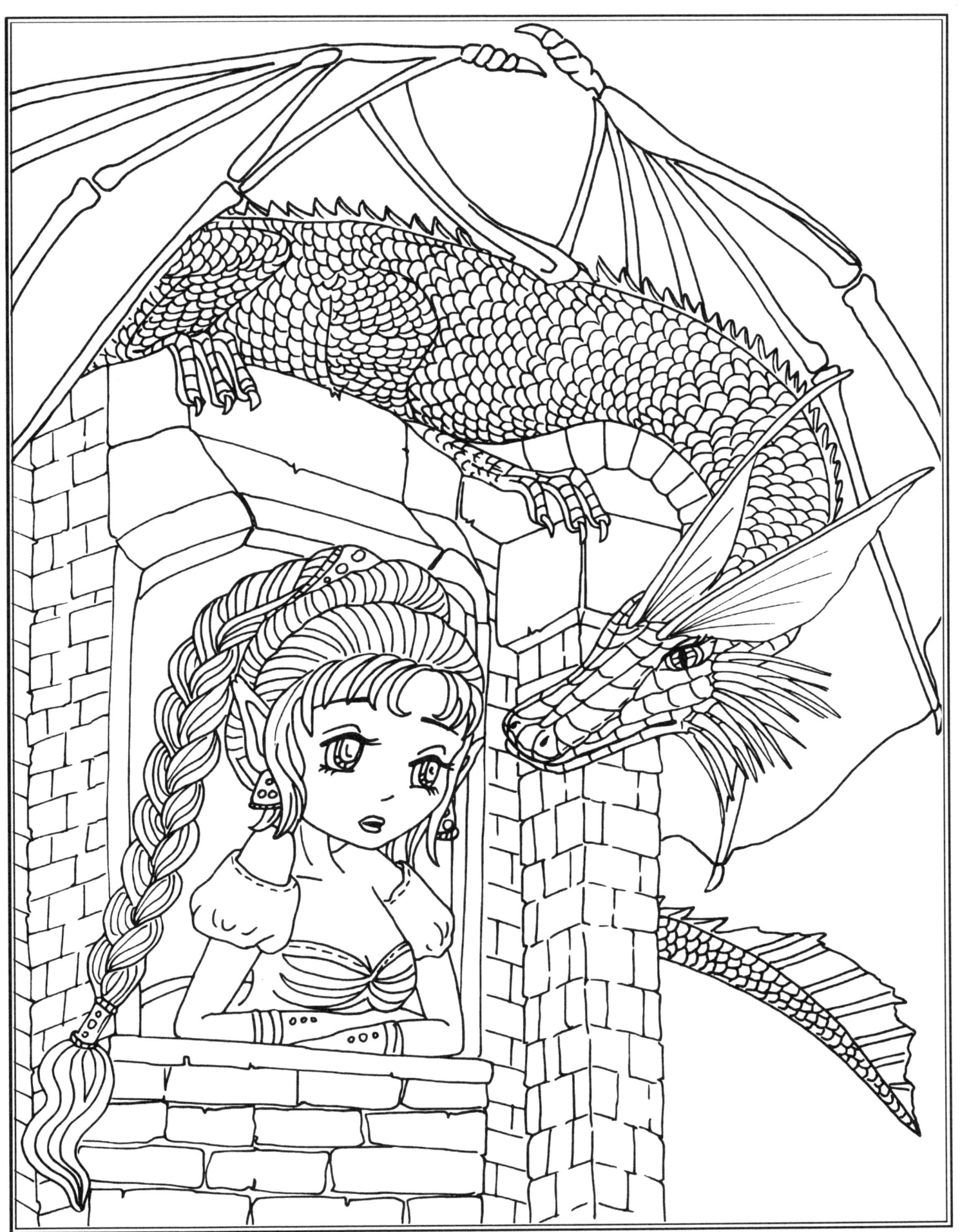

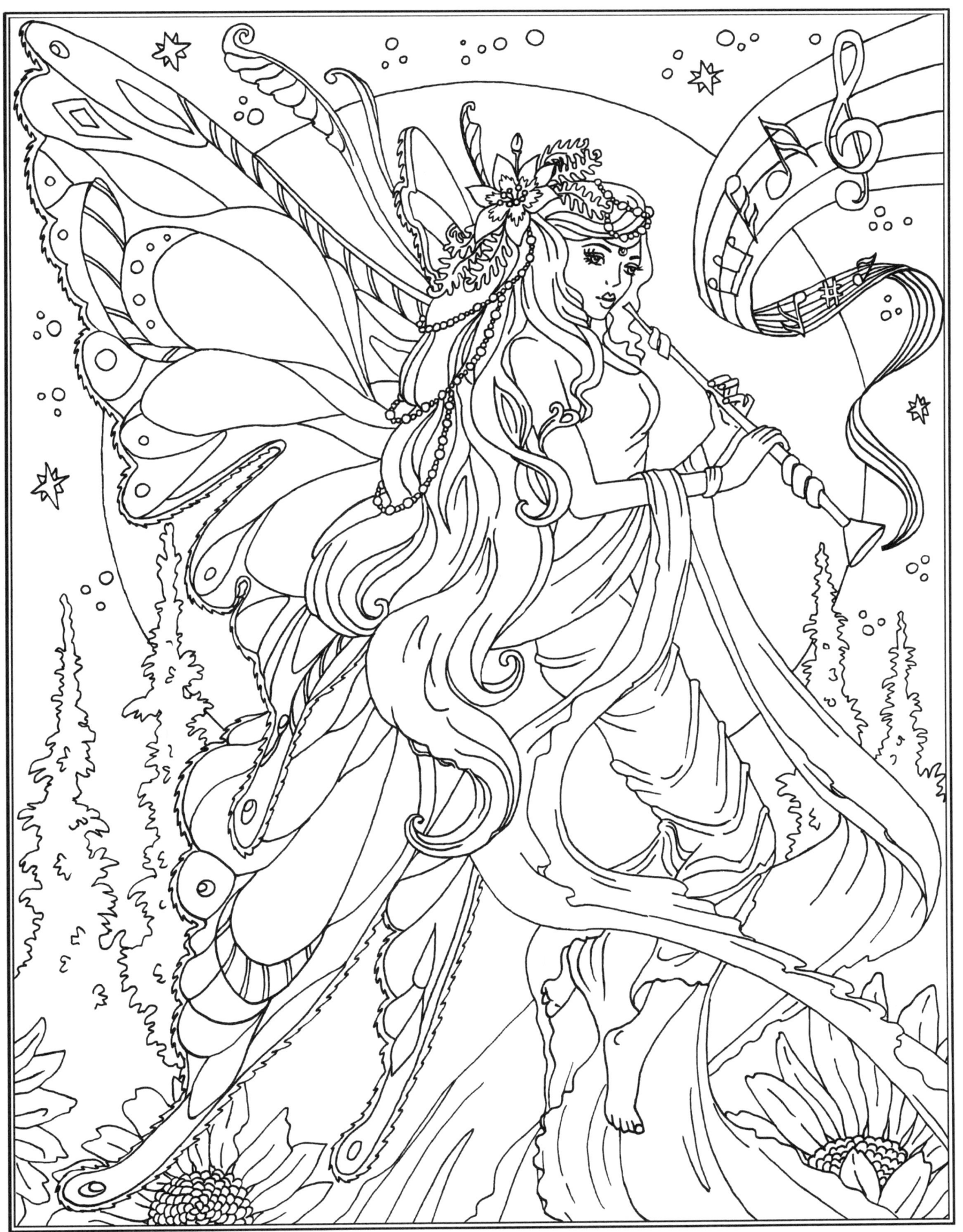

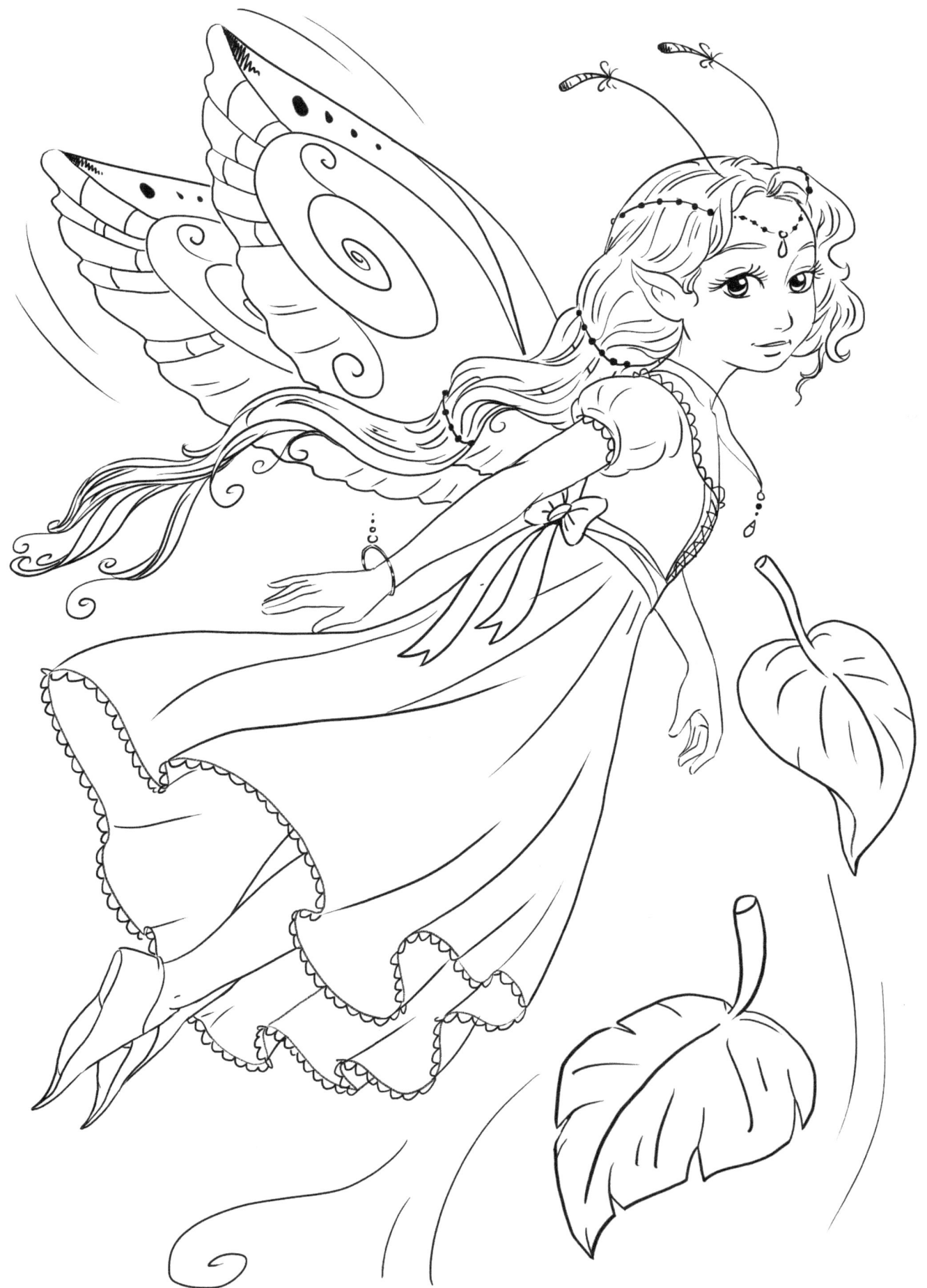

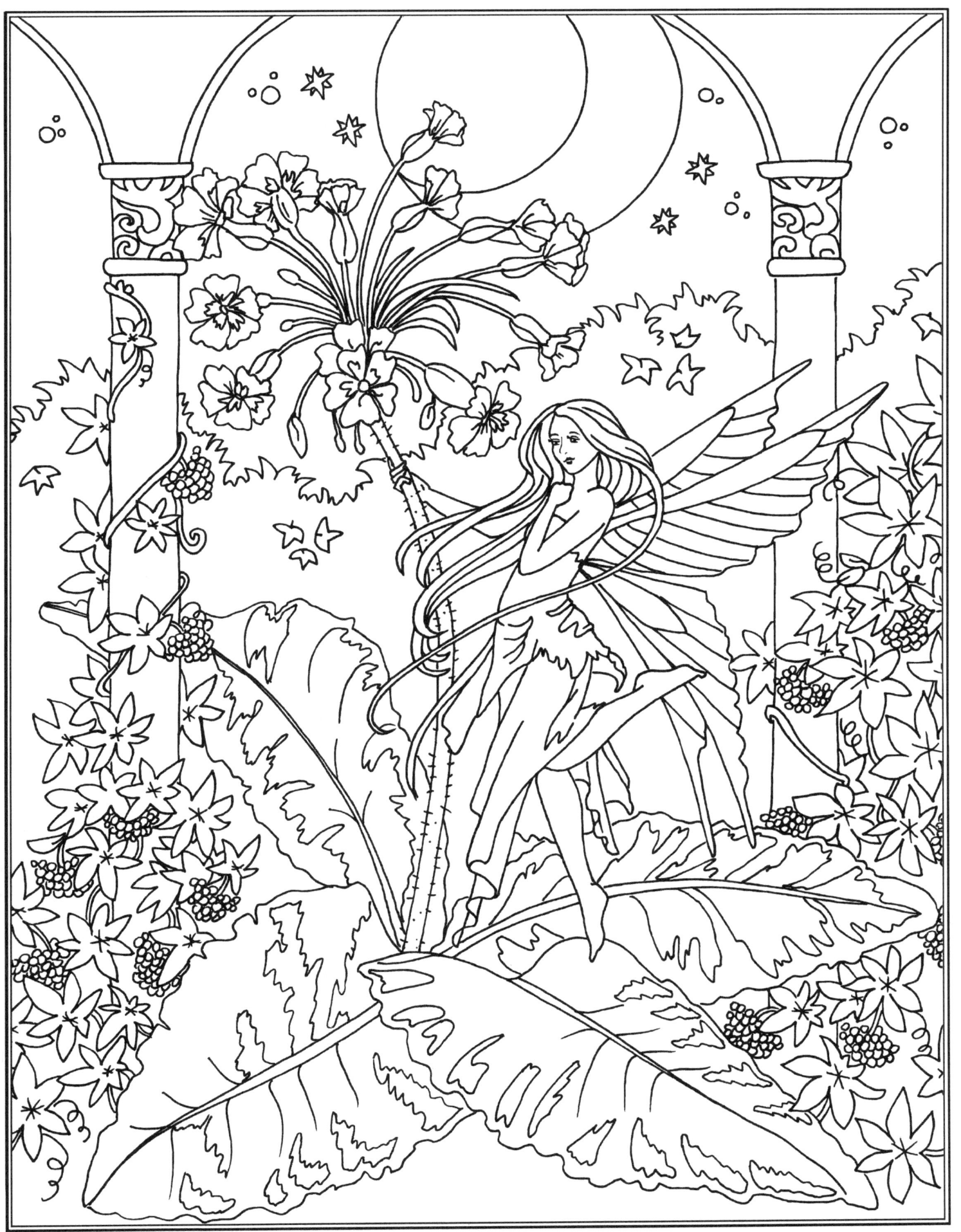

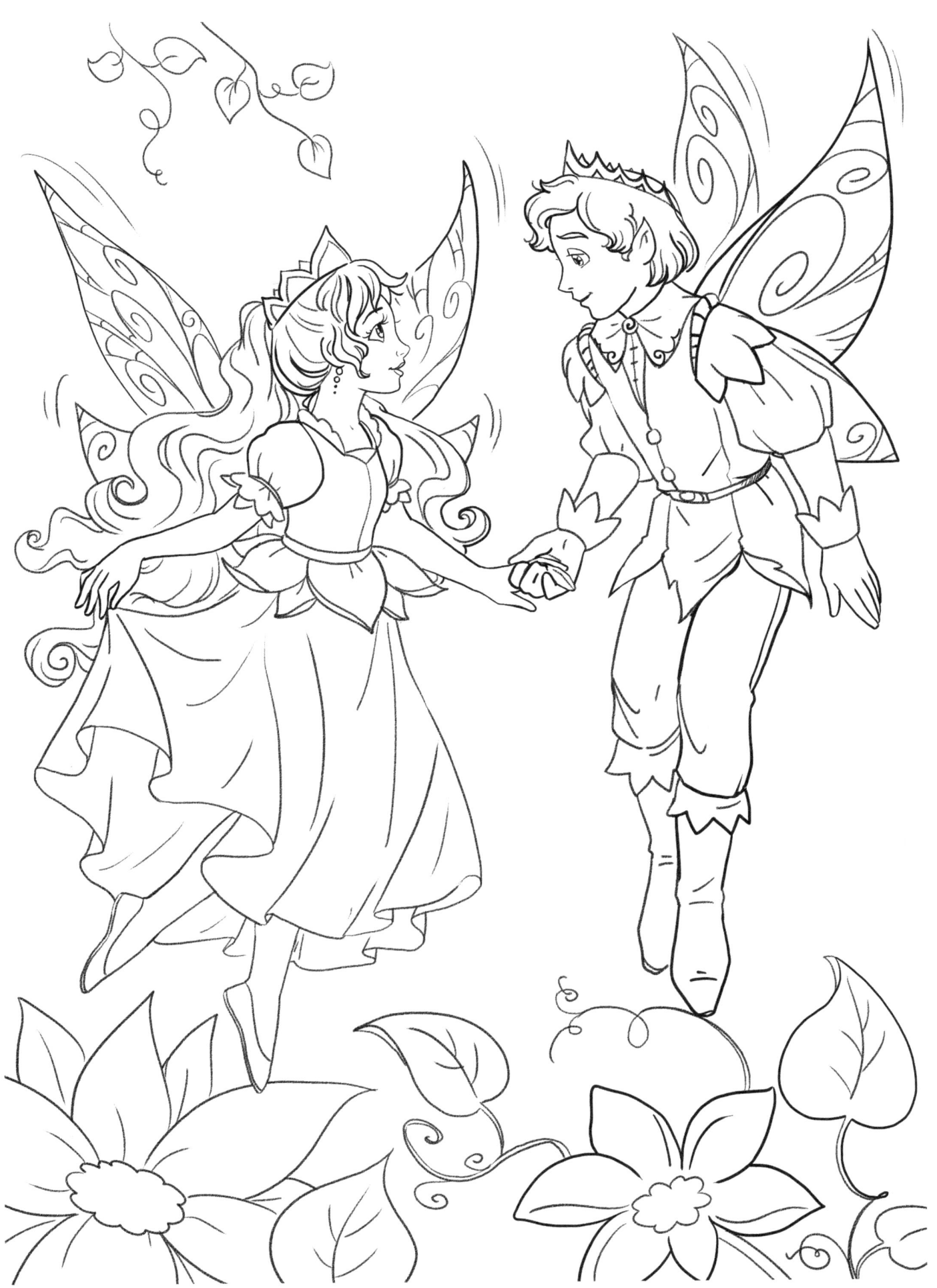

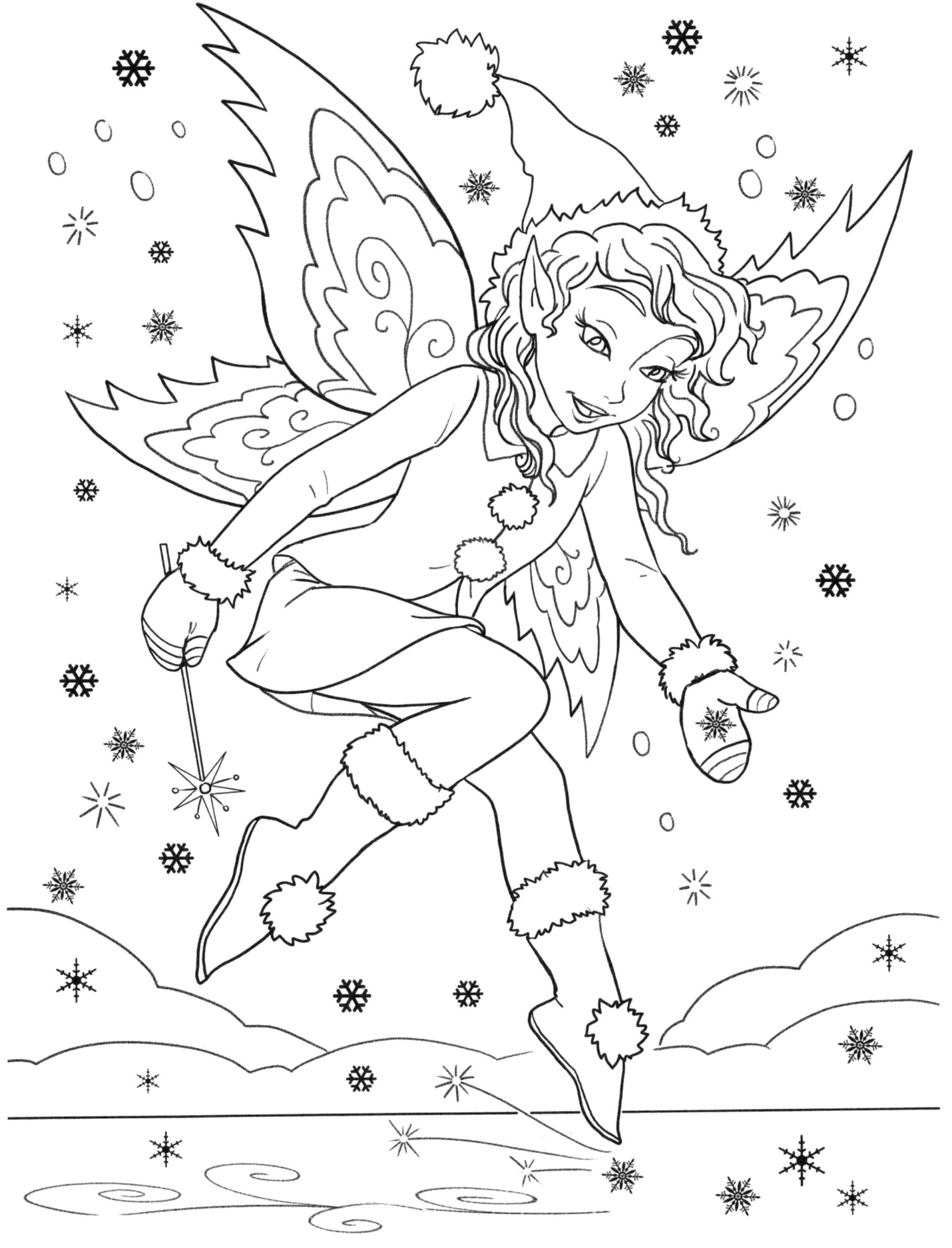

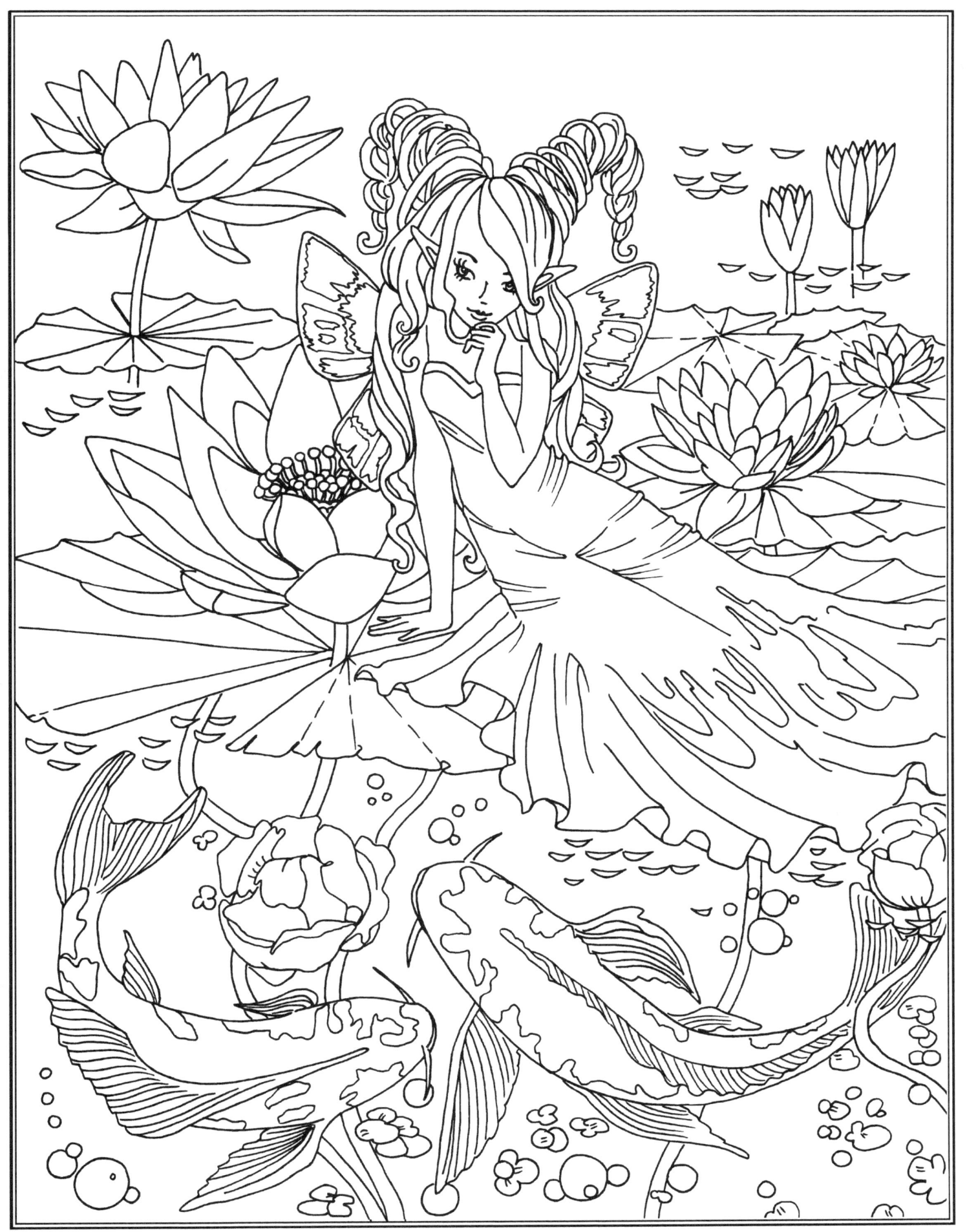

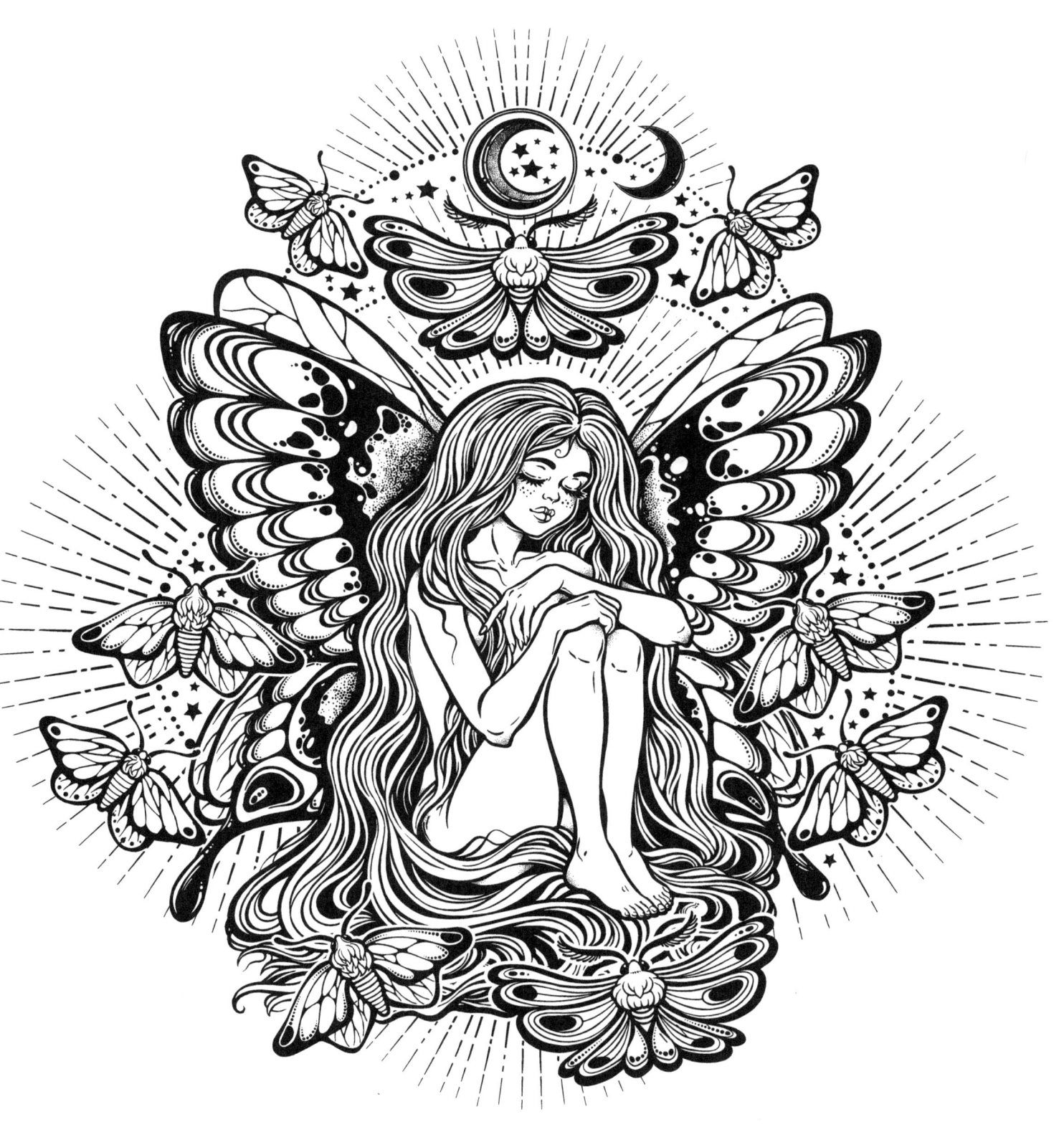

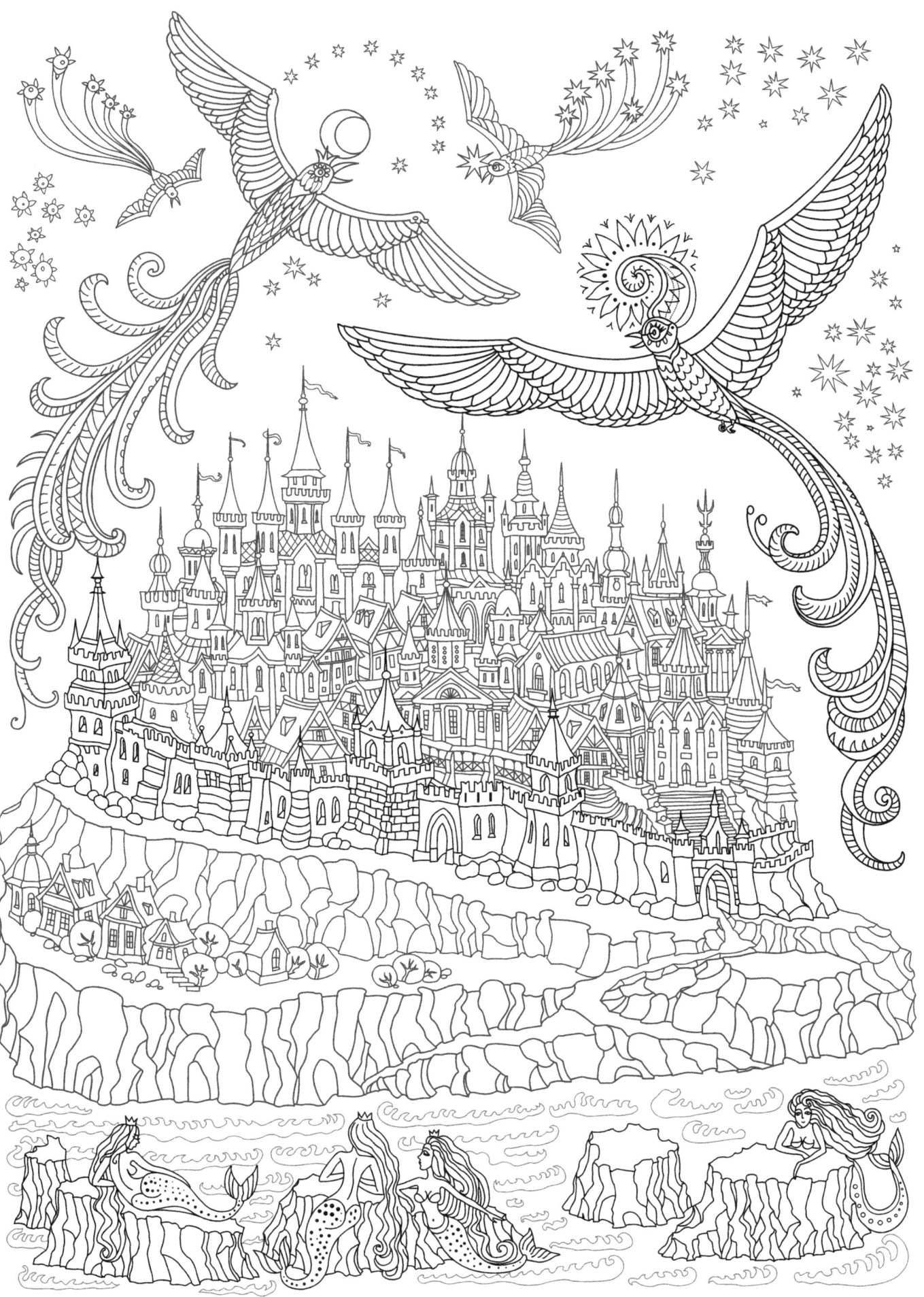

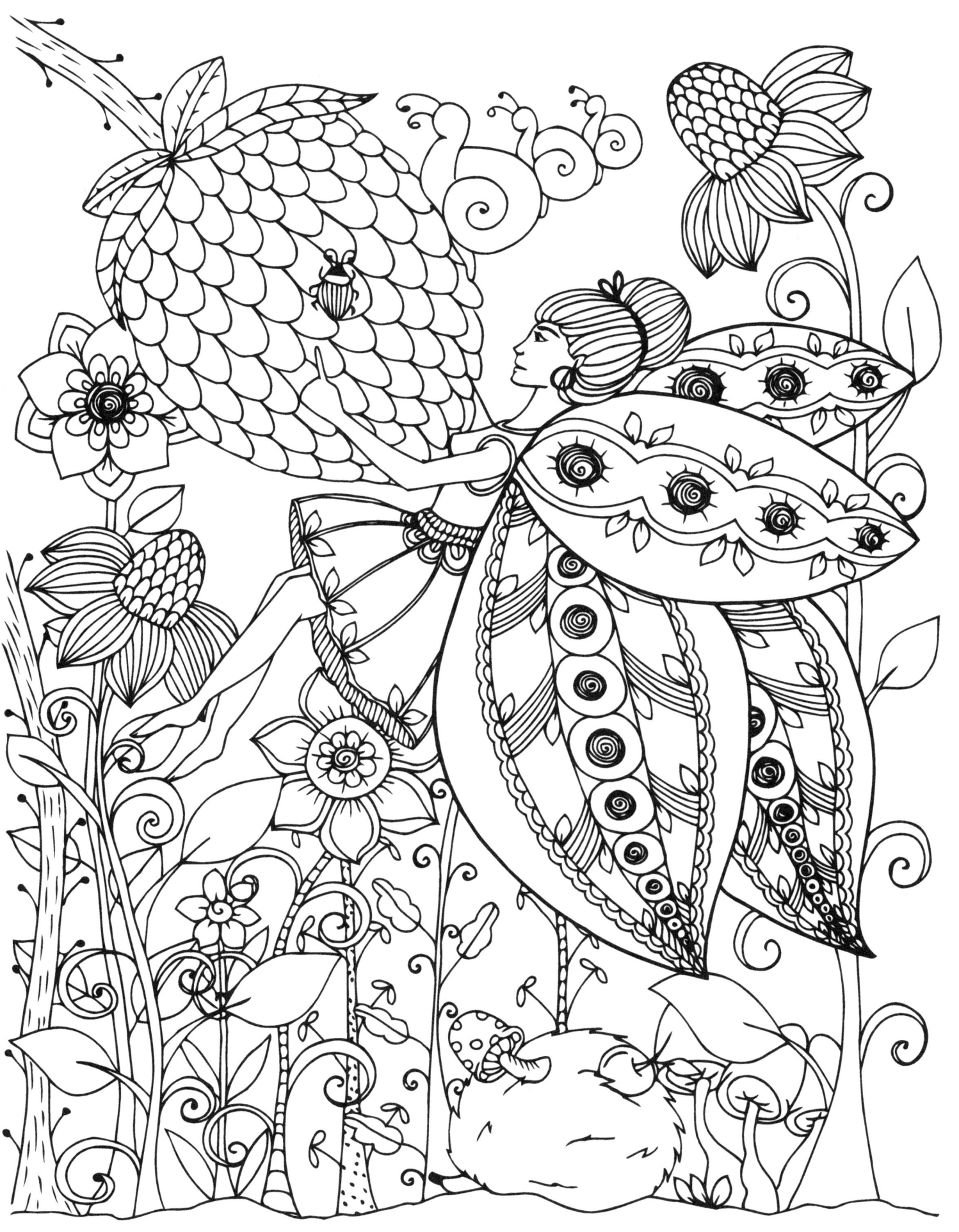

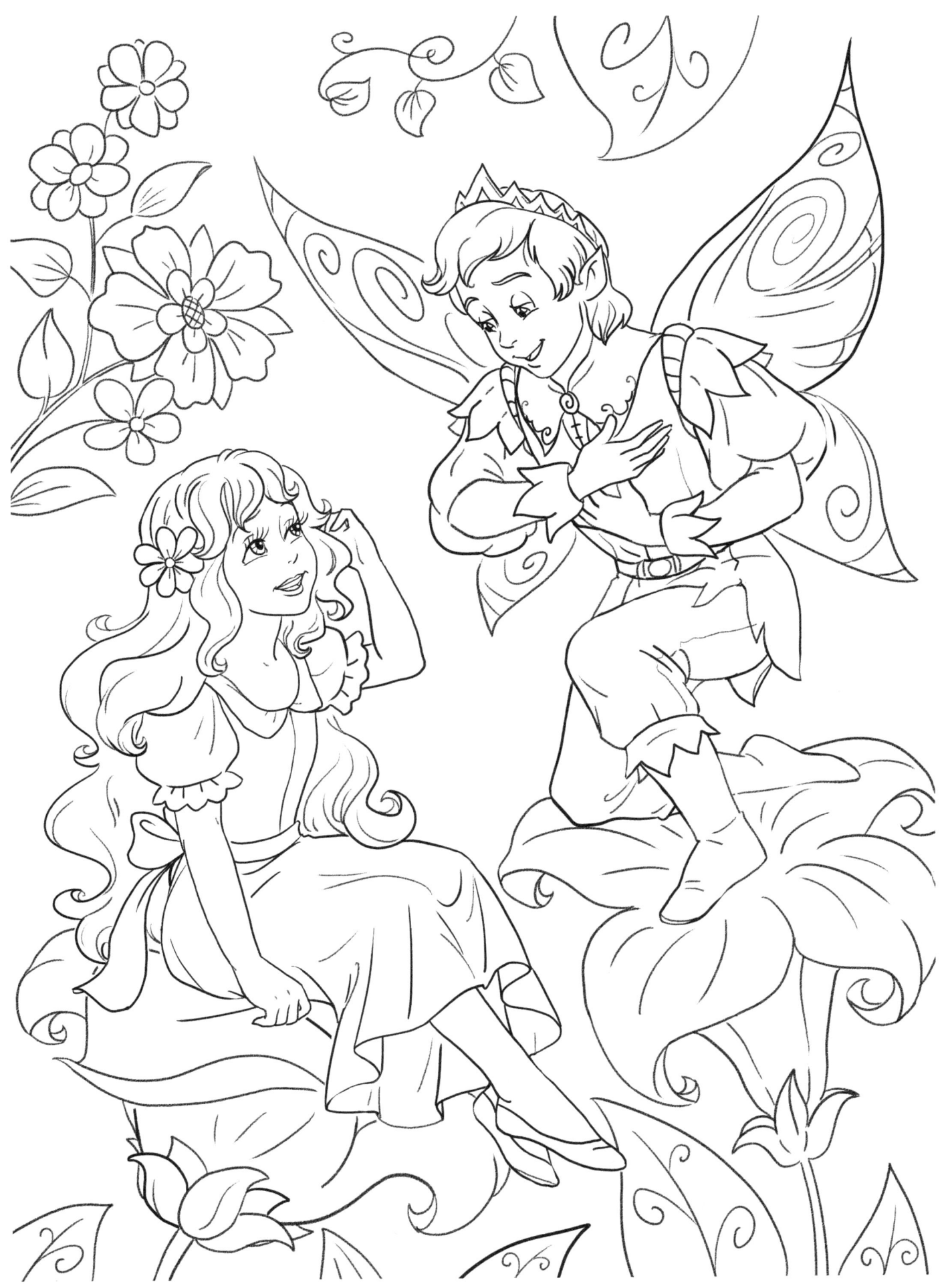

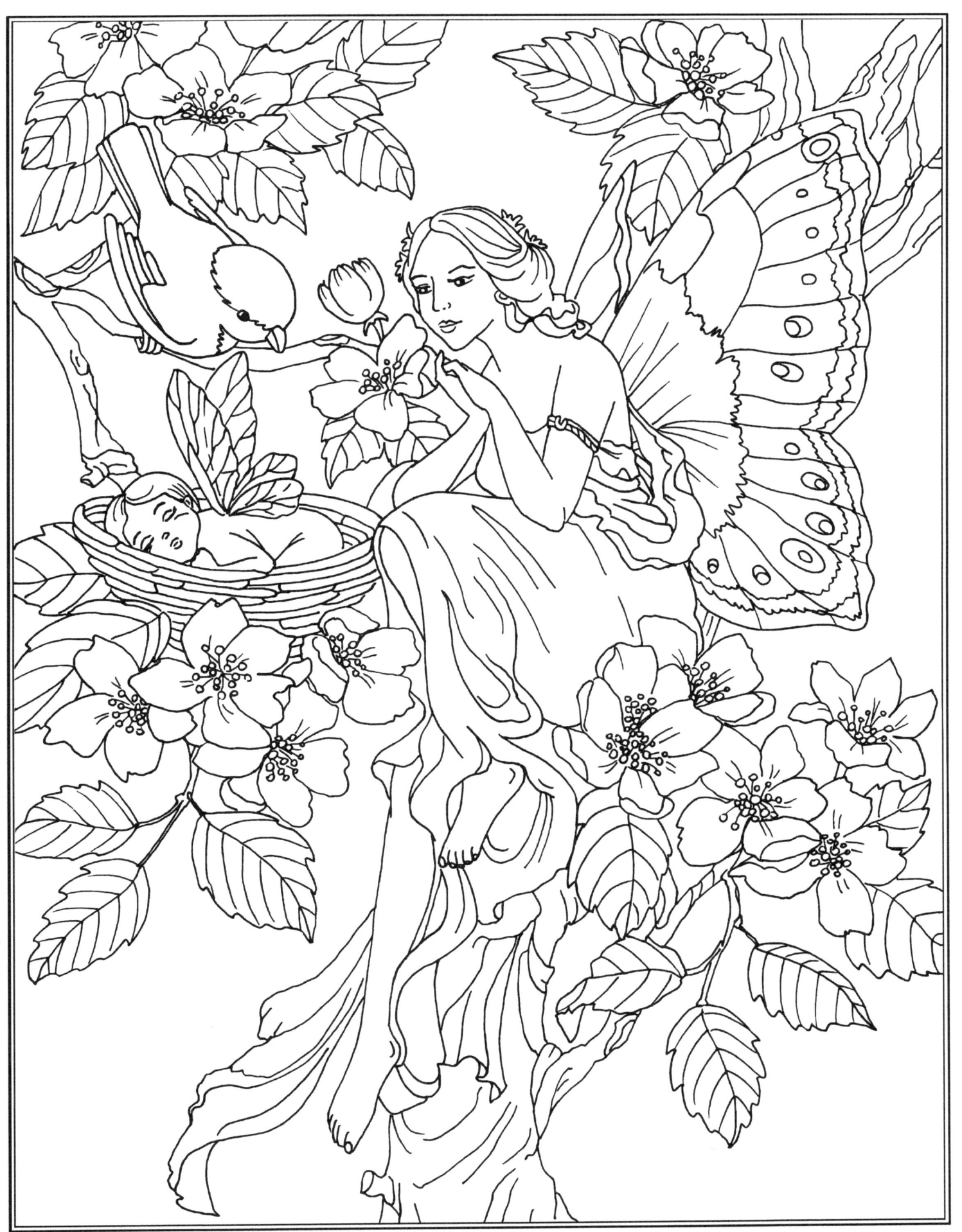

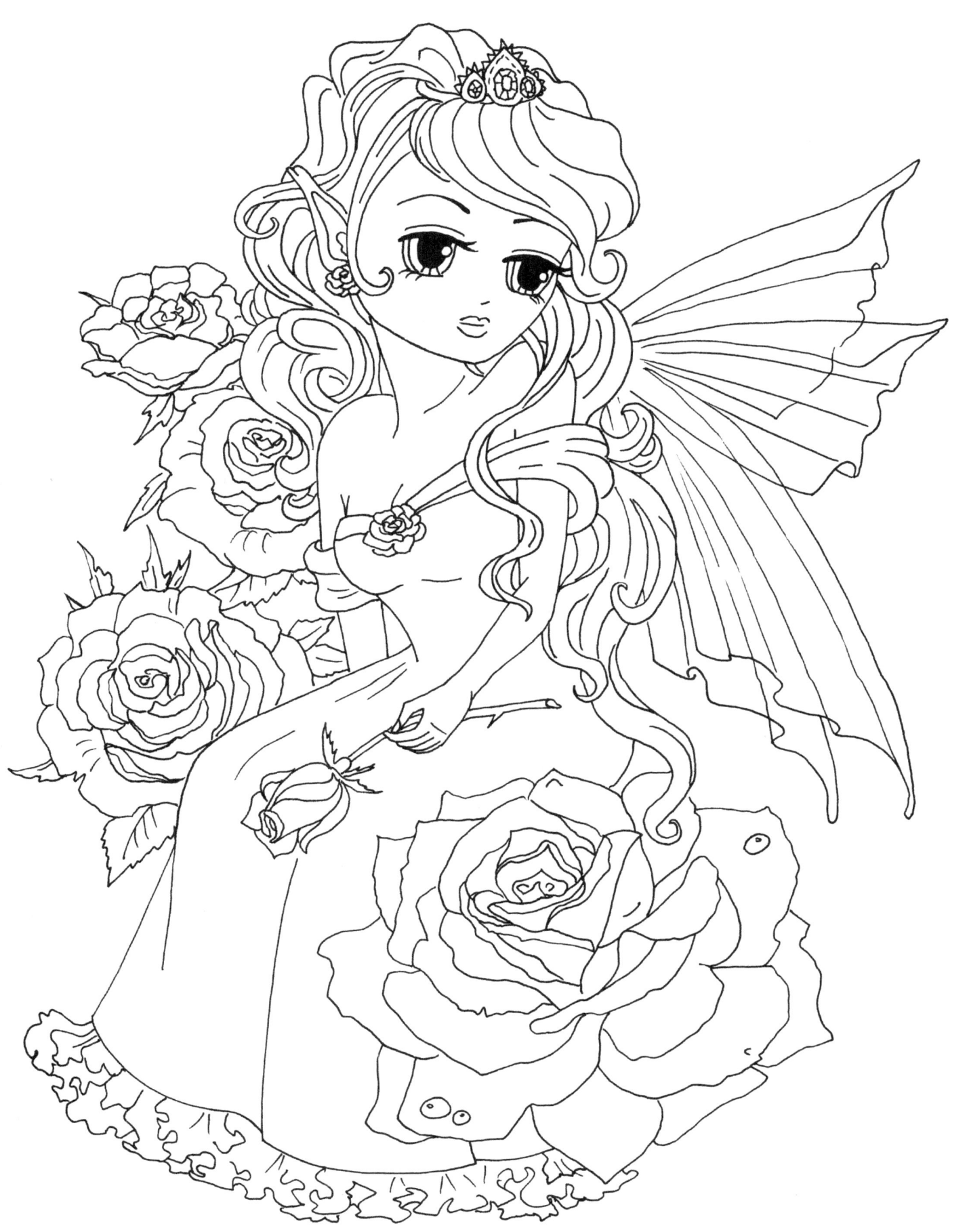

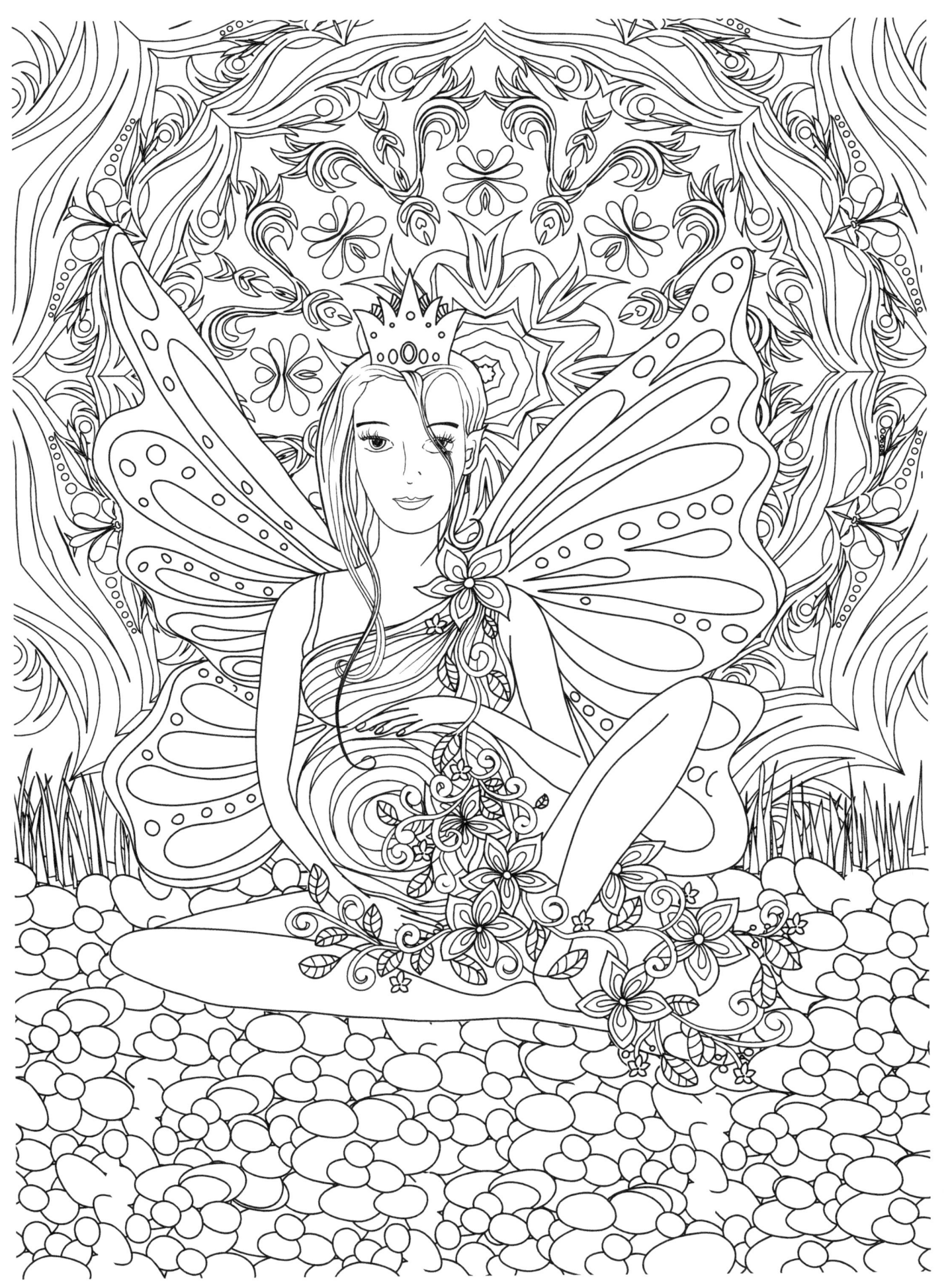

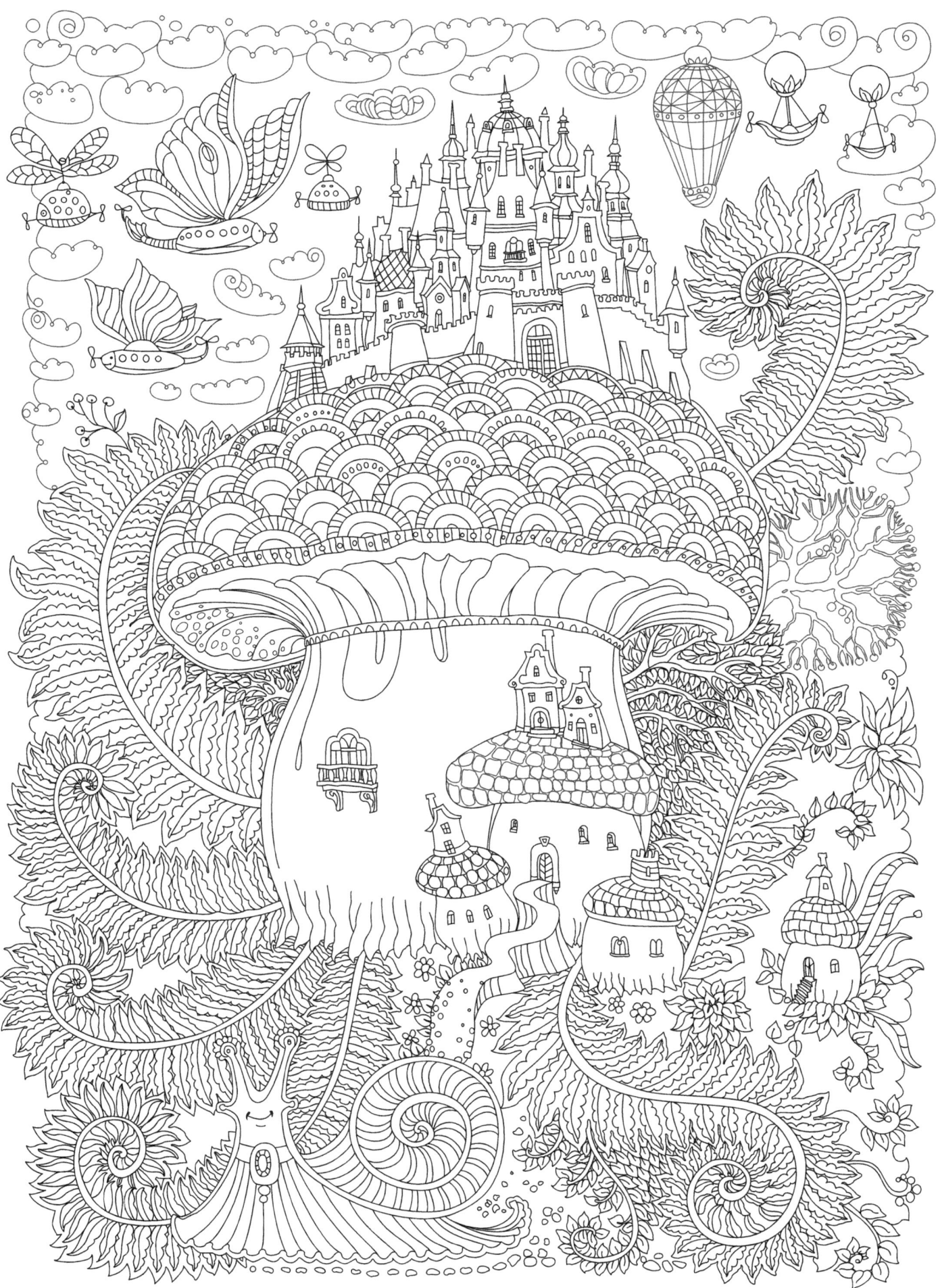

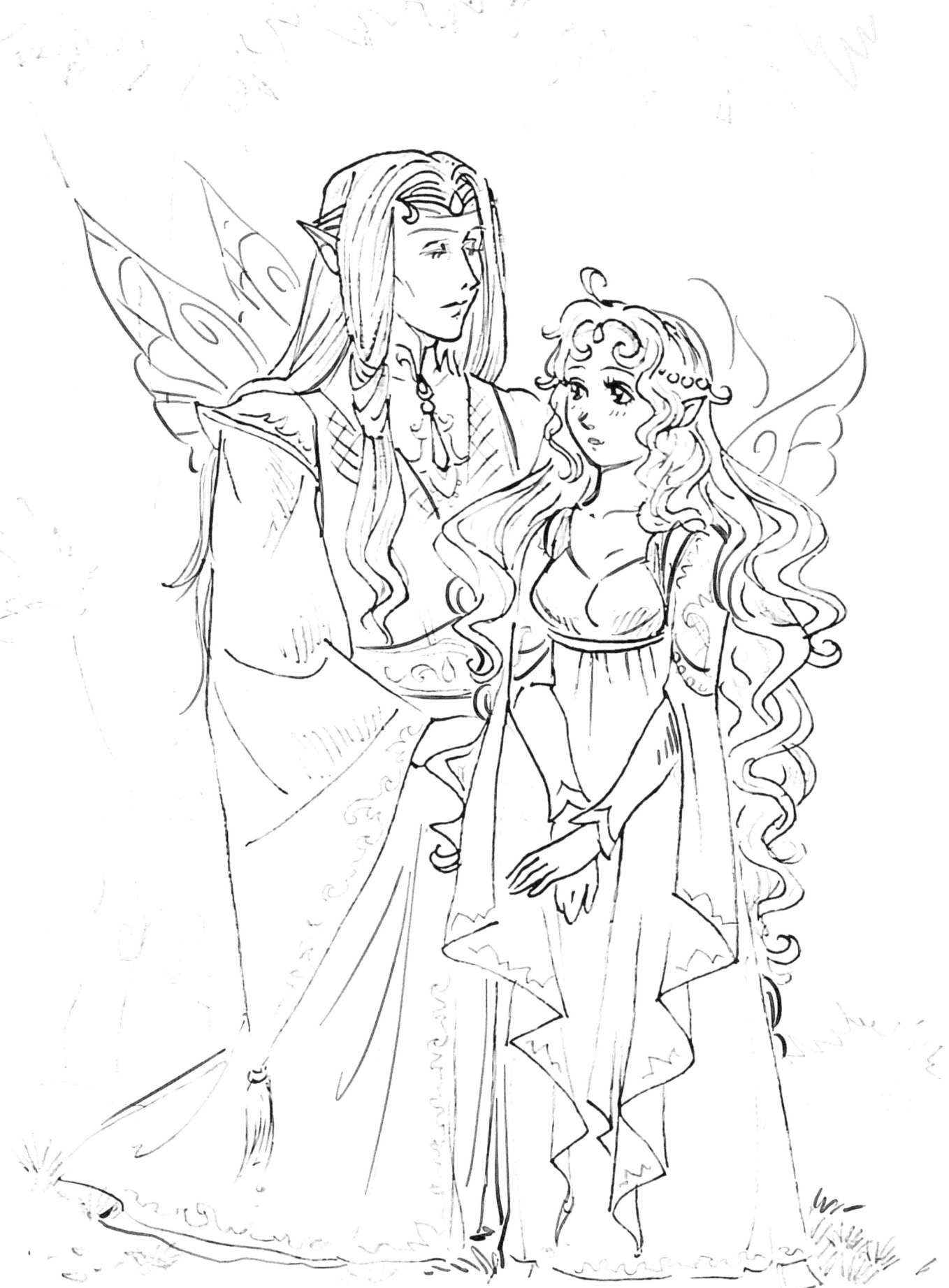

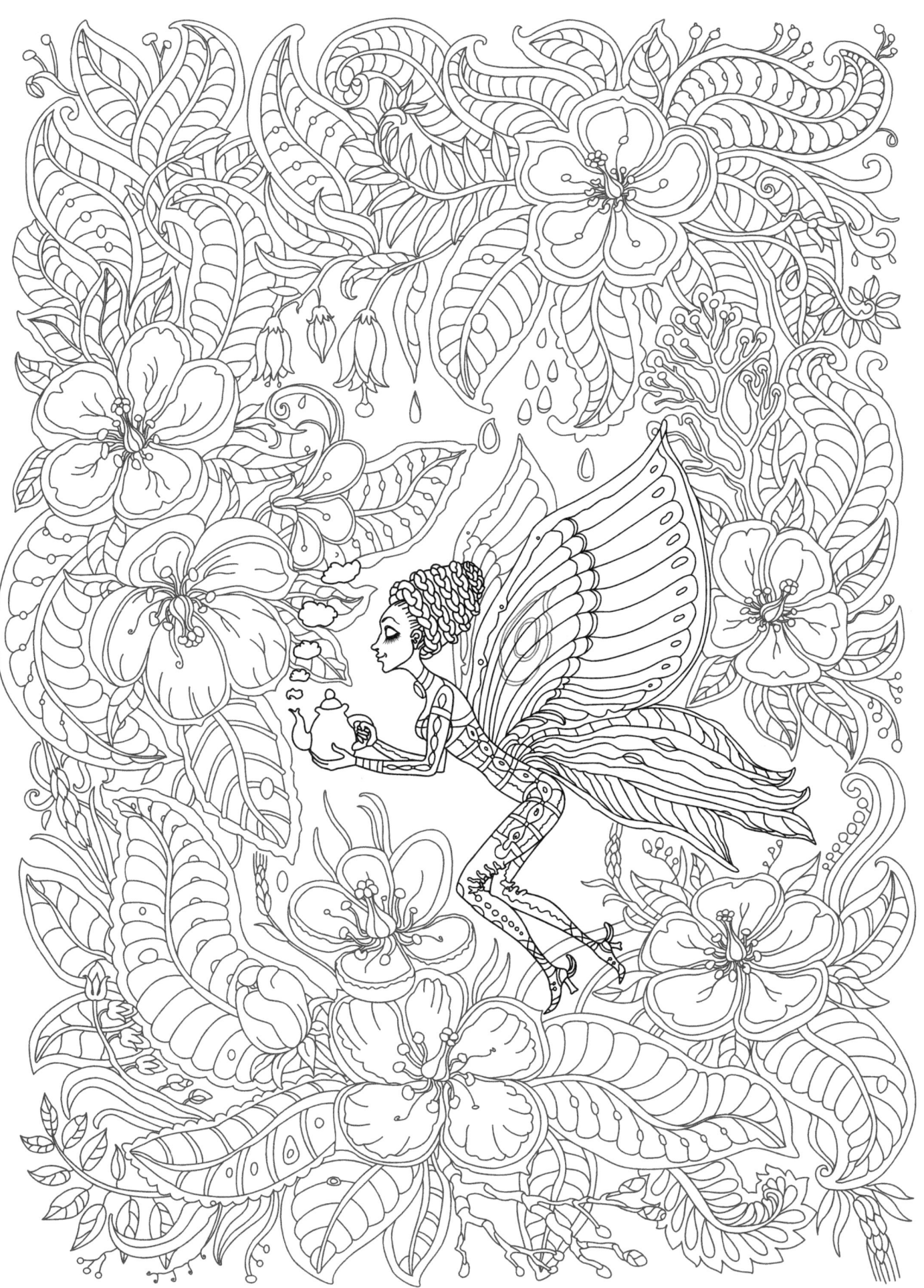

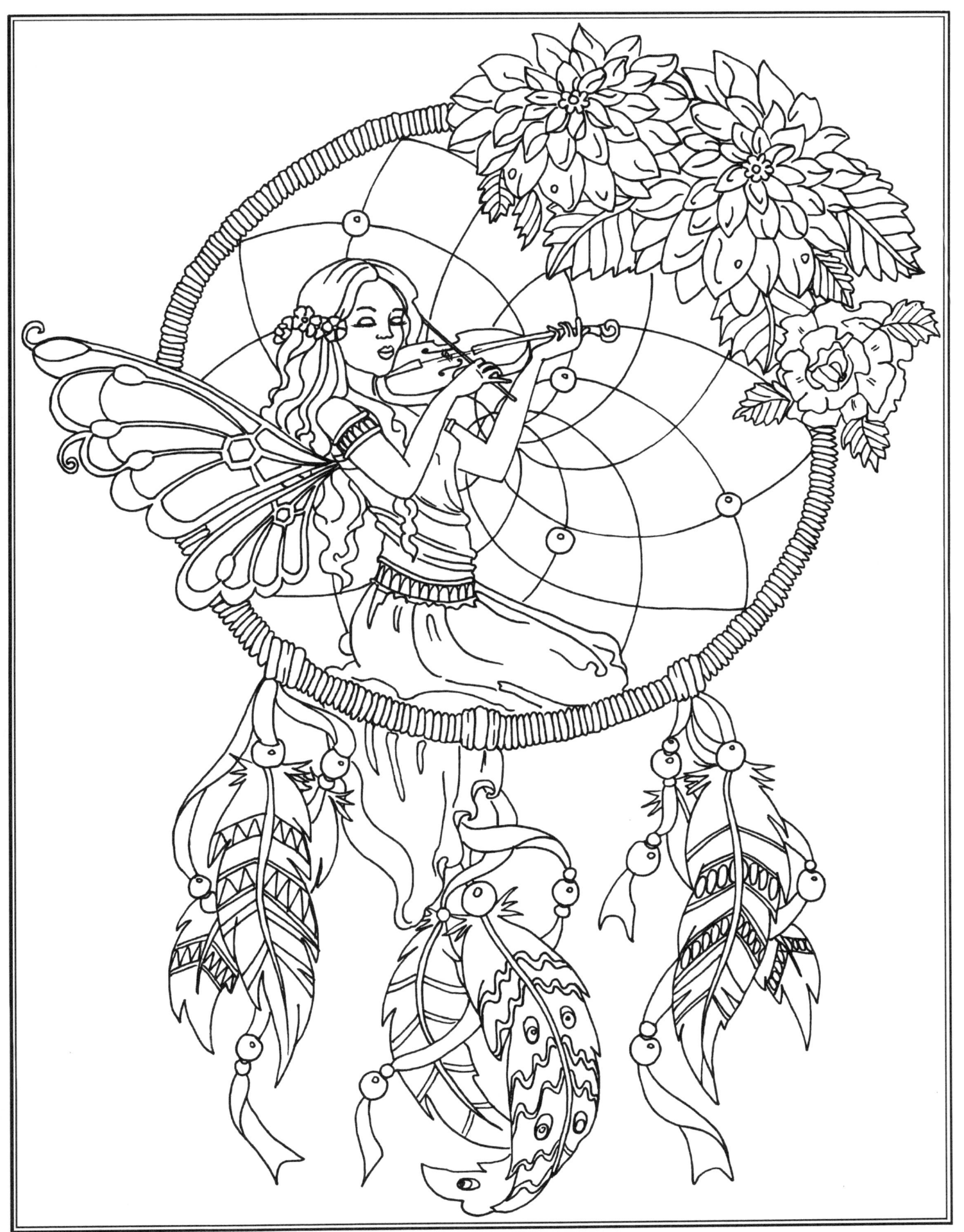

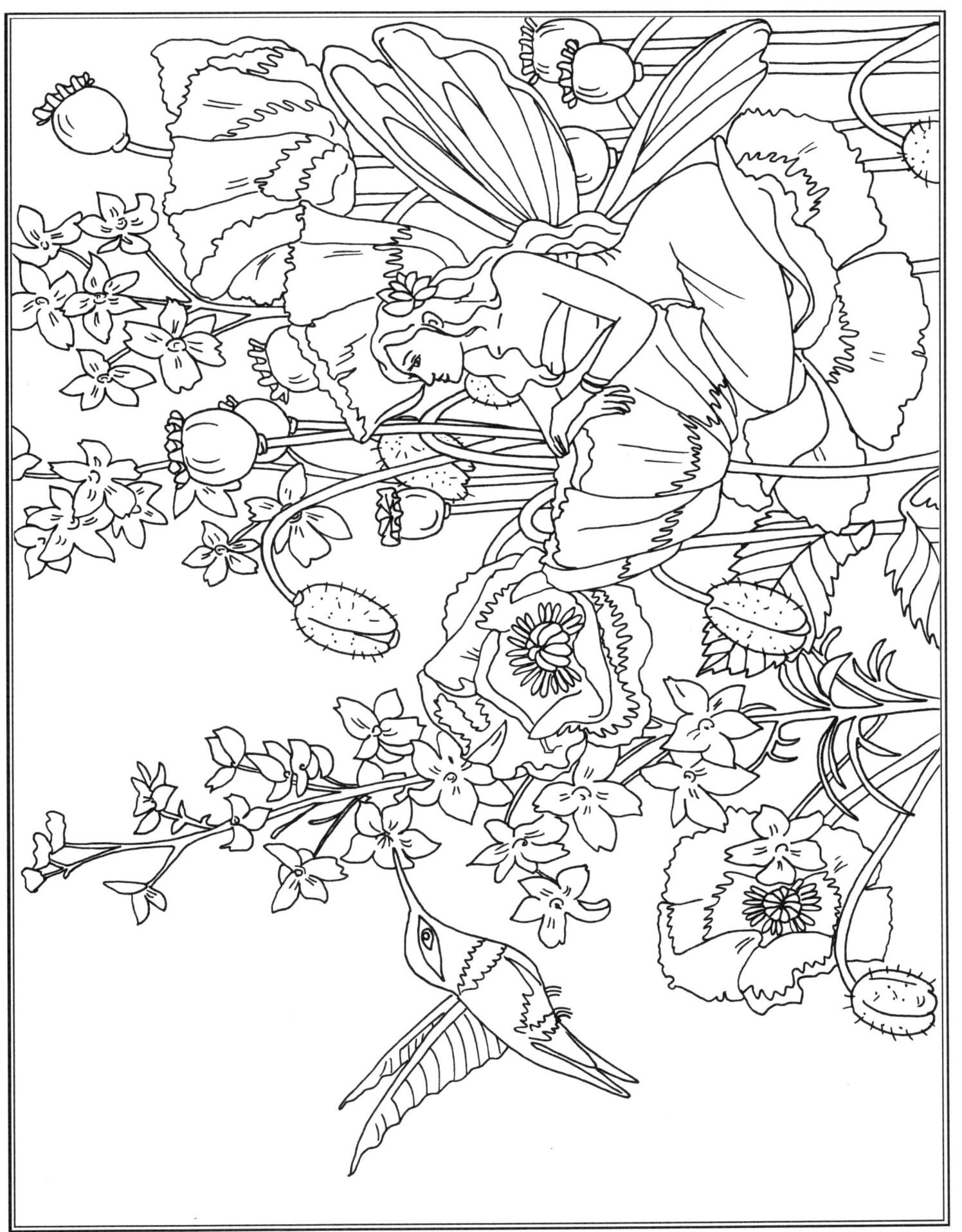

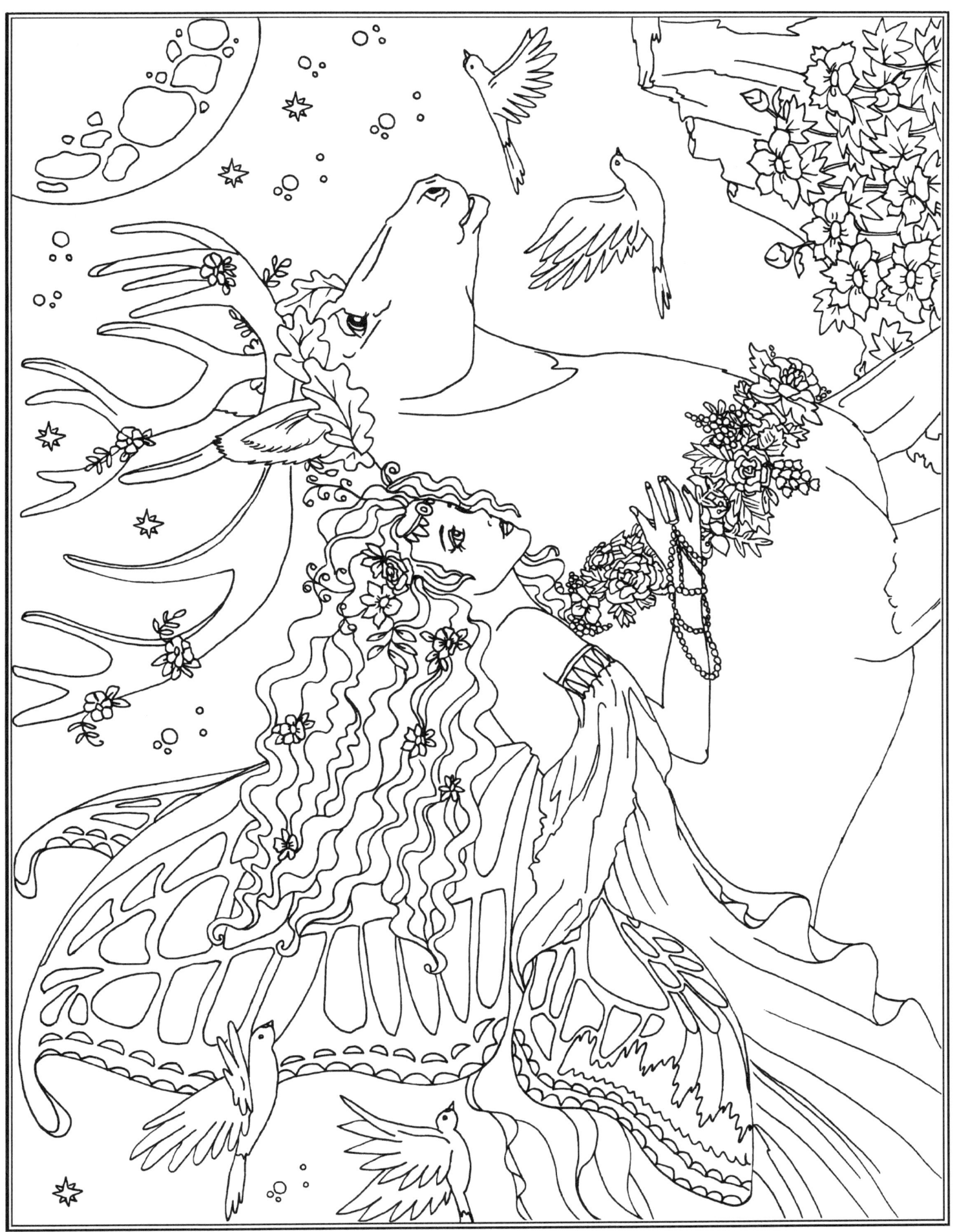

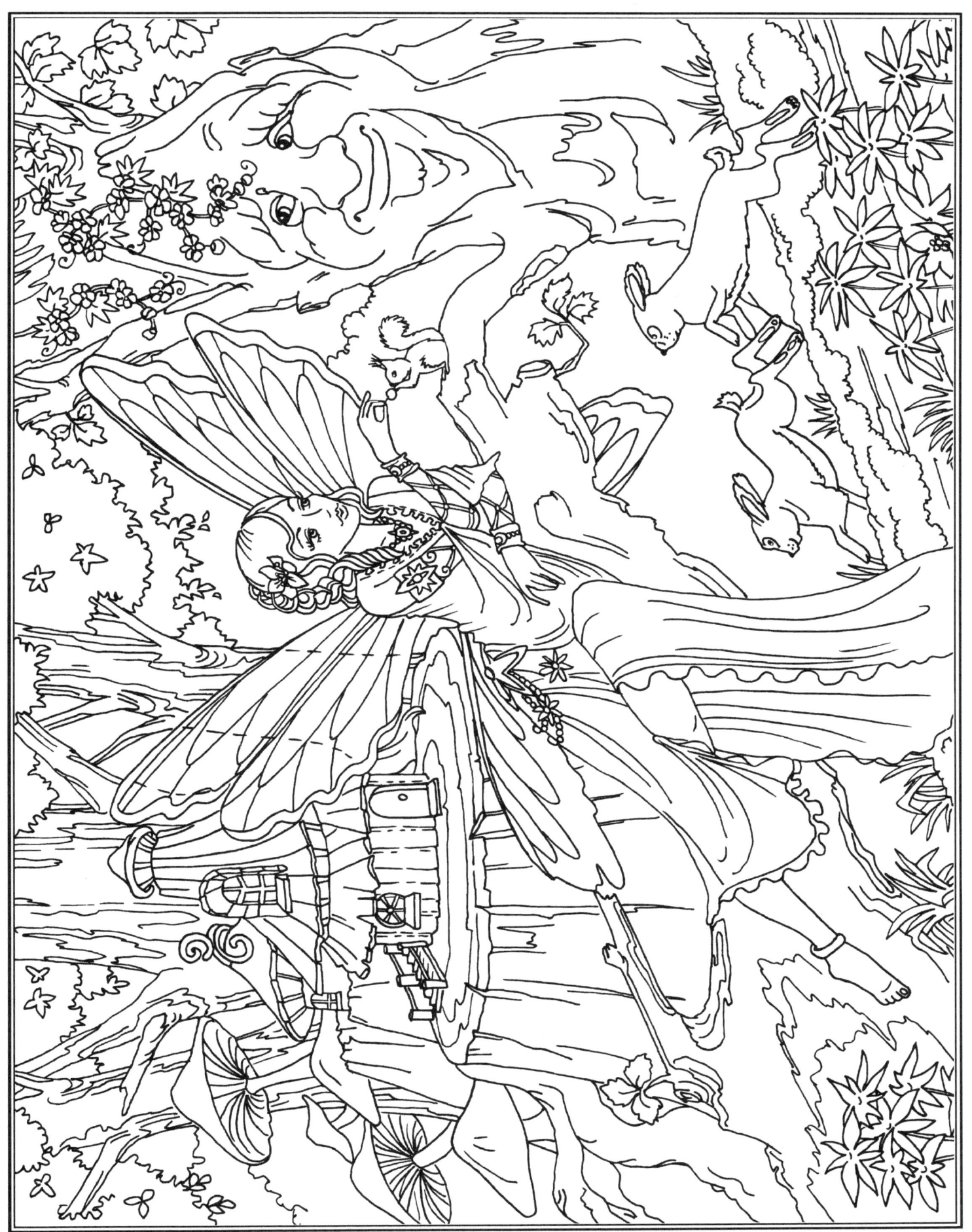

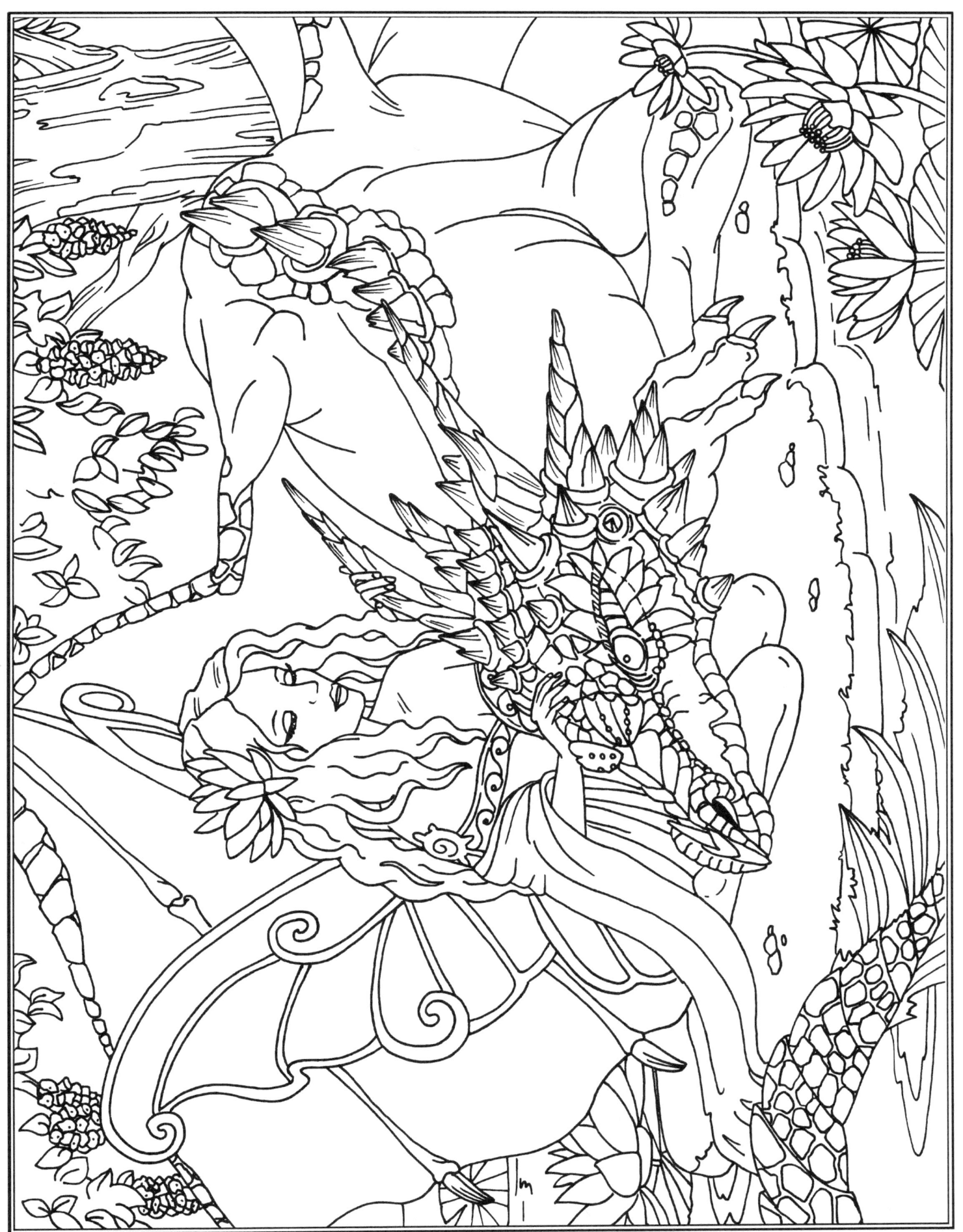

www.ingramcontent.com/pod-product-compliance
Lightning Source LLC
Chambersburg PA
CBHW060000230526
45472CB00008B/1884